Across the Blanket

Gordon Brocklehurst

First published by Badgerwood Publications in

2003

Published November 2022 (v2)

Profits from the sale of the republished
version of this book will be donated to
Barnados

First Published by
Badgerwood Publications LLP

ISBN 9780954508722

Dedication:

To all Old Barnardo Boys and Girls

Journeyman Weaver

A promise not kept remains a promise; the passage of time may change its interpretation, but not its essence. This particular one was made almost casually, rather than solemnly, but the occasion remains clear in my memory: it was 1966; Dr Barnardo's Homes were approaching their centenary celebrations; a great meeting was to be held in London, and the reporters were out and about, looking for stories from those who were known to have been boys or girls in the Homes, and had subsequently achieved something in the world outside. They found in me a young doctor, impressed by their attentions, but pre-occupied with the task of becoming a brain surgeon. They wanted to know how I had got thus far, and although I gave some kind of outline of my course since leaving the Homes, there was much I did not tell them: how I had to change from being a successful member of a Barnardo Nautical School, destined for a life at sea, to become a public school boy; how I found my way through a privileged education system to a place in a great university, where I not only studied medicine, but many other things; how, in due course, I moved on to a renowned hospital, where I became deeply involved in the process of becoming a doctor. Nor could I tell them how it was that my form of doctoring sick people became that of a surgeon, and that I had already served in the army as a Surgical Specialist, with the rank of a Major - for when they found me I was starting again as a lowly House Surgeon, with a greatly reduced salary and a growing family, all to enter neurosurgery. I was particularly concerned at that time to avoid becoming the object of any special attention in the press, for I still had a long way ahead to reach what I knew to be a demanding professional role, and I was anxious to maintain an impersonal relationship with patients in general, and with my mentors in particular. The reporters left with only the

1

bare essence of a biography to include in their articles, and they promised not to use my name, while I, in return, promised that I would one day relate the full story myself.

Some seven years later, I had reached the main objective of my endeavours, and was poised on the edge of discarding them all. In a profound change of personal relationships, I had turned away from my beliefs, aspirations, family, and friends. I was then alone for a while, and, by way of reflection, took to writing of my plight - but it made heavy reading. The person who remained closest to me at that turbulent time, said it was premature to write of my life, and, when I most bemoaned my state, reminded me of the privileges of my profession. I was also told that I had chosen rather an obvious title, but of that I did not repent, for the euphemism, like the more gentle reference to being born out of wedlock, or the frank word illegitimate, expresses society's response at the time of my birth, but with the connotation of conception - an act for which I remain for ever grateful. However, a saga of sad introspection was not a worthwhile biography, so I turned back to my responsibilities, and sought the philosophy whereby I could best practise what I had so painstakingly learnt.

Looking after patients, both day and night, then became my pre-occupation, for this was already in the nature of my speciality, and I adopted it. The promise remained, but so did the justification in not keeping it - the yarn was still being spun and my experience was changing. That which I had seen as a vocation of caring for people became a service for patients that also involved administration, research, and teaching; these were the elements of a busy professional life and the determinants of my personal reflections. It was some years before I returned to writing down my private thoughts, but, by the early 1980's, I had sketched out a structure with which I could work; thereafter I made the occasional reflective note or alteration in the outline.

The following decade included an experience that could not fail to influence my biographical inclinations. Ideas do not come entirely out of the blue, one might say in these days of psychological insight, but on that particular morning in Sancerre the sky was certainly cloudless and this odd thought came apparently unheralded. We had been travelling for some days along the Loire valley, searching out the origins of some well-known wines, and had found many of the vineyards tucked away between the villages and the yellow fields of sunflowers. We had sampled a bottle or two, here and there, from the caves or outhouses, and finally, on the previous evening, reached this little town. The room, in which we had slept so contentedly, was on the first floor of a pension at the corner of a street leading from the town centre. When I pulled the curtain aside to let in the morning sunshine, the empty square could be seen to the left, and across the street was a bric-a-brac shop with a few prints in the window. It seemed worth getting up and clothed to walk across and look more closely, in case there was a subject, style, or engraver of interest, but there was nothing to add to the few simple decorative pieces already purchased on this French trip. It was on turning away to face the sun across the square that the thought of four people and the fifty years since the time they were together in one of Dr Barnardo's Homes quite suddenly occurred to me. It was so vivid that it is tempting now to look upon it as some revelation from without were the unconscious powers of a shop-window image, a brilliant sunny Sunday morning, or the rich river of thoughts which flows so easily when travelling abroad, to be disregarded.

Whatever the origin, the thought grew. Initially, it was a concept only, just as it had come to mind on that memorable morning - a quartet unaware of itself - but I held four threads, which could be brought together again. Let me explain.

Firstly, there was Kenneth: tall, freckled, with auburn hair - an upright character - who was promoted to become a Leading Seaman well before I was. We were at Russell-Cotes Nautical School - a Dr Barnardo's Home that trained boys for the Merchant Navy - and when we first came alongside each other were still under fourteen years of age. He was in Howard House, and I in Arranmore. We were called 'elementaries' in a school where most of the boys expected to stay on, as 'nauticals', until the age of sixteen, and then go to sea as apprentice deck hands in the Union Castle Line. Ken and I already knew our seamanship as well as the ordinary schoolwork, and were shaping up to our future at sea. In the classroom, he was also ahead of me, until I caught up, and then beat him to the top. It was at this point that we were both put forward for a scholarship to a public school, which sounded grand and very different from where we were. The place was given to me, and Ken stayed at the Nautical School until, at sixteen, he left to become an Officer Cadet in one of the great shipping lines, and finally a Master Mariner, while I went off to Bryanston, and was educated sufficiently to become a doctor. Perhaps it was our juxtaposition at school that started the friendship; it continued throughout our different lives. In the earlier years, we quite often saw each other; we shared an involvement with the Church, and, when we had children of our own, with our family lives.

Of Morgan I can say little about the time together at Russell-Cotes, for he not only was in a different house, but also appeared to be a different kind of boy. He was handsome, dark, and strong enough to be independent of other friends. He made a successful bid to join the Royal Navy as a cadet from our Nautical School, and that was notable since the Barnardo Home which primarily trained boys for the Royal Navy was not Russell-Cotes but the Watts Naval Training School, in Norfolk, reputed among us to be very much stricter than our own place. Morgan

4

and I remained in contact through the friendship of Peg Dovey, a gentle lady whom we had known as a Matron at Russell-Cotes, and, through her, we remained friends with each other. I saw him occasionally during his course, which went from the Royal Navy, to university, then to teaching, and the career of an educational psychologist. Our friendship remained and grew somewhat stronger.

Colin, on the other hand, shared the same house and many interests with me at Russell Cotes, and we became close friends while there. He was stocky, with black curly hair, short legs that served him well for both football and gymnastics, and a marvellous gift of music. There was never anything nautical about him; he seemed to be visiting Russell Cotes from a real home elsewhere, rather than belonging to our institution, and this I liked in him. We played in the Nautical School band, were both good at gymnastics, and spent hours together on the hard asphalt playground. He never stayed to become a committed nautical, but left at fourteen to learn a trade at the William Baker Technical College - another of Barnardo's vocational training establishments. Our close friendship lasted for only a short while after I had gone to my public school; we met once or twice in the holidays, and then no more for many years.

It was shortly before the Loire valley trip that Colin found my address through the Barnardo Guild and we met again. His life had been spent in the business world, laced with a certain sporting excellence, and his remarkable ability in music. The same friendship was there, unaltered by the lapse of time. The warmth of this renewal may have surfaced on that sunny morning in Sancerre, when I thought of the four of us with a shared long past, and, by good fortune and some tenacity, the threads which still linked us.

We then met as a foursome, under Colin's auspices at Birmingham, and found the common ground of our beginnings was still there. In the subsequent year

5

or two I prevailed upon the others to set down an account of their life within Barnardo's and thereafter, for I was convinced that the experience we had shared in one of Dr Barnardo's strictest Homes some fifty years earlier had remained throughout our very different lives, colouring our response to others, and to ourselves. We were a quartet, defined in a different epoch, and now re-gathered in the present era of reflection.

Then came the BBC programmes in 1995, entitled: 'Barnardo's Children - the biggest family in the world'. It presented on our television screens an extraordinary display of old Barnardo photographs mixed with sufficient live interviews of an oddly assorted bunch of ex-Barnardo people to promote the themes of forced separation of related children, and repression of information about them and their families. Later episodes featured the discovery and re-unions of long separated families, more to the benefit of investigative journalism than to the participants, I thought.

It was my conviction that Dr Barnardo had provided homes for children otherwise not cared for by parents or society, and the measure of his particular methods of institutionalisation, fostering, or deportation of these children must be the success or otherwise in changing them from being unloved to becoming loving beings, which is no easy task. Conversations with my three companions from Dr Barnardo's Homes increased this conviction, and I was carried away with this concept of a Barnardo Quartet. For a time I even saw us as playing our respective instruments, with the overtones of our personalities while we put together our composite experience. Among themes of struggles, tensions, achievements, and failures, all developed from our start together, I could see form, even whole movements, but I could not make the right composition, and I did not fully understand the music. My companions, meanwhile, had sought out their Barnardo records, and increasingly

6

pursued the ramifications of these, while I continued to miss the dialectical nature of what we had all endured in the change from being the unloved to becoming the loving.

As a child I regarded the little which I knew of my own past as irrelevant to the present in which I was endeavouring to live, and, as a youngster at school, I thought the discussion of such personal matters was in poor taste, but I never overtly denied them. By the time I was shown the file which contained my own Barnardo records, many years ago, I was already an aspiring sapling, and roots were not very much in fashion. When I grew to the stage of branching out to bear fruit of my own, my roots, as I knew them, were made known to members of my family; I have also shared them with a few intimate friends.

I was not, therefore, a participant in the rush which occurred, following the BBC programmes, to seek out long-hidden Barnardo records. Of their value as sociological history, I have no doubt, but to replace longstanding happy or unhappy ignorance with personal information of potentially devastating significance has required from Barnardos a diligence well beyond customary aftercare. The factual revelations from my own Barnardo file had not changed my reticence over my origins, nor did the recognition of their psychological significance, as I began my medical education. Christianity taught me self-acceptance, avoiding both embarrassment and notoriety, and I balanced knowledge, insight, and inclination, with a little help from others, to carry my past with reasonable success.

The direction of my clinical training, along a course in which the necessary discipline of neurology predominated over that of psychology, increased the reluctance to relate my own personal behaviour as an adult to my childhood as an orphan in Dr Barnardo's Homes. Maybe this pre-occupation with the treatment of the very system that subserves behaviour lessened my attention to behaviour itself. The delving by our quartet, on the other hand, ultimately showed me that the origins which we had shared coloured the personalities we displayed in our relationships with institutional authorities, competitive society, close partners, and, ultimately, with each other.

An account of my roots, and of how I came into Barnardo's, was not included in the promise that I made to the reporters, but it would be an inadequate story without it.

There are many people, both well-known and less so, who, having been children in Dr Barnardo's Homes, have made their mark in later life, and a few have written their accounts, but I know none who have become doctors, with a ministry similar to that of the Homes' founder. It is a profession privileged to participate in the life and suffering of others and, with this, reflection and authorship have come frequently enough to produce a great band of medical writers; perhaps I might aspire to join these.

However, the particular form of doctoring undertaken by a brain surgeon is demanding, sometimes dramatic, and frequently devastating. It takes many years to reach a degree of proficiency, and its practice then becomes an exclusive pre-occupation. Its practitioners are more likely to be written about than given to writing. It is a speciality within which I can make claim to endeavour, rather than to pre-eminence, and, although it has been arduous, never have I felt distant from the many people whom I have treated, nor from the deep desire to practice my particular craft to the best of my ability. In the first respect, I have sometimes been too close for ethical comfort, and in the second, suffered the price of disregarding both my colleagues and my family; such hazards of my course should be charted.

Nor could I keep the promise while I was in the midst of such a clinical life, but now that I am able to reflect upon it at some distance, deferred questions come to the fore:

Is the story of real interest?

Can I write it?

Will anyone read it?

A positive answer to all three might justify its publication, but I cannot follow Mark Twain's advice and defer some aspects until after my active life, and others for a further fifty years for fear of producing hurt or offence; I must avoid the first, and risk the second only when justified.

Furthermore, I cannot emulate those gifted writers who have presented their experience of Barnardo's in memorable prose, for my writing has been primarily for clinical and scientific ends. My account will incline, therefore, towards the description of personal relationships and situations. With neither the pen to tell an entertaining tale, nor the brush to portray a colourful picture, I must rely upon what art there is in knowing how people and places have been woven into my person to become the strands of caring and concern for others. I could, perhaps, draw out some of these as the warp across which I have plied or been plied, and offer this - as much a garment as a story.

Should the hand of Dr Thomas John Barnardo be discerned within these patterns of the unloved and the loving, I shall have kept my promise.

Lily May

She was a small and gentle person. From the beginning, I knew that she loved children. Her black hair was usually made into a bun at the back of her head, but I knew that it was really long, for she would sit before her dressing table in the afternoons and comb it out while she talked to me of when she had been in service with a family in Bedfordshire. She had been nanny to their three children and related times of a good home life and happy holidays. Her fondness of the two small boys in the family was clear. A portrait of her taken when she was with them hung downstairs in the living room. It showed her seated, half facing the camera, a slight figure dressed in a pale blue cardigan, and the thick black hair gathered up neatly around her head. On the other wall was a much larger picture in a heavy wooden frame which portrayed a demure girl in a white dress and bonnet, adorned with pink ribbons, sitting with her gloved hands held piously together in her lap; beside her a bunch of cherries. The family had given this picture to her when she left and to me it spoke of the gentility that she had brought with her to our little home at the upper end of the village.

The nearby town of Watlington is small and sleepy. It nestles alongside the Chiltern Hills, a few miles southeast of Oxford. The ancient tribes that passed along the top of the hills on the Icknield way would have overlooked it as they went. The country roads that reach it from many a small village, including our own, must have brought travellers to and from a busy market place in earlier times, but now all is quiet.

At the time when I was brought there, almost seventy years ago, the Great Western Railway reached it, but only just; a single track left the main line at Princes Risborough and wended its way alongside the hills until it ended at the station, a mile or so from the Town Hall.

I know that I came with someone from Dr Barnardo's Homes, and was handed down from the train to my foster parents, having brought with me little but three memories of earlier childhood; they have remained ever since, unaltered, unconfirmed, but not unlikely.

In the first, I was among the audience in a big dimly lit theatre and on the stage a woman climbed into a box, and then disappeared. She returned to the stage from the back of the theatre on a pulley along a rope above the audience. In the second, I was being taken around a park that had a large floral clock on a bank side, and when the hands reached the hour, a nearby cuckoo came out of a little door and proclaimed it. The third was more domestic: I was playing with a silver netted ball on the end of a piece of elastic when I lost it over a high fence at the end of the street - I climbed up to look over and I saw a train thunder by in the cutting below. When I returned to the house there was an older boy unwrapping a parcel containing a uniform, which I associated with the Navy. I was aware of being called by my name - Gordon.

As for the rest of the first five years of my life, it was a jumble of faces and places, which I was willing enough to exchange for a home with a Mum and Dad.

Our foster Dad was quite big and bluff. He belonged to that part of Oxfordshire, and when they married, in 1919, after he had returned from being in the army during the First World War, they had a short stay in another village before they settled into one of the houses newly built by the council at the upper end of Cuxham. They had two boys of their own and took in two more from Barnardo's. It was said that they had hoped for a family of four and, when she could not have any more herself, they made the family up with us. It could have been so, for one of the first two boys from the Homes was, she said, 'so naughty' that he had to be sent back, but she always related this fact with such a wistful smile that I felt that she really loved little Jimmy Parker, despite himself.

11

I was the replacement, and proved good enough to stay. A year or two later, when Jeff, the other foster son, reached fourteen years, and was reclaimed by the Homes to be taught a trade, he was, in turn, replaced by another boy called Terry, as though the family was always to be kept to four.

The village was small, and even as a child you knew most things about most families. A few had been there for generations and, like our neighbours on both sides, were related to each other, but no friendlier for that. Others had less direct relationships, and sometimes their children had a different name from one or other parent; some children lived with a single parent.

Our house had two rooms downstairs and a small pantry. There were three bedrooms, no bathroom, and the lavatory was outside. We lived as a close and happy family and I knew the other families in the village, and the lanes, fields and brooks around it, in the detail that fills a small boy's life.

The road to Watlington had banks on both sides where it passed our house, and on the one opposite to us was the pond of an old mill. It filled by a brook, which came down from the Chiltern Hills and ran round two sides of Nixey's field on which was the cricket pitch, fenced off in the centre, with the pavilion at the far side. Beyond this, another field sloped up to a skyline of straggly fir trees, visible from our front room. Only a small amount of water from the pond trickled down over the millwheel; the main flow was down a waterfall to rejoin the brook.

The mill was built of brick surmounted by boarding painted a light brown, and it was set back sufficiently far from the road for an owner to have posted a black-lettered notice saying 'No Parking Here' which I associated for some time with a tasty brown cake which our foster Mum cooked for us. I thought of the mill as a mysterious place, whether you viewed it from underneath, alongside the mill wheel, or over its roof, from the top of the great yew tree that grew up against it. At road level its front was a plain brick wall with gates at the right side which led to the part used for loading and unloading in the long- past days when the mill had worked; we climbed round the gate and over the bridge to get to the cricket field. To the left of the main building a long flight of stone steps led up to the front door of the house which was set even further back, at the height of the pond; it was this relationship of building to the water at the different levels which made it intriguing.

There was a particular dank smell to the immobile old wheel embedded in the sand of the brook which, at this point, having been diverted through the pond and millwheel, returned to its meandering course through the village. Normally this was a quiet stream which flowed alongside the village street, almost to the far end, before it crossed under the road and on to the Far Meadows, where it contributed to the water-cress beds, and to the swampy fields where the rushes, wild irises, and king-cups grew. It must have started somewhere up in the hills beyond Watlington, for when the snow on these melted, after one severe winter, it swelled to such a torrent that, when it reached our village, it by-passed the raised mill pond and flooded down the road in front of our house. We sat at our front bedroom window and counted the groups of ice fragments as they flowed past.

There was a time when the cricket field had been kept mown and was used by the village team for matches, but I suppose the active men became involved in the war; the fence around the pitch broke down and it joined the rest of the field, to become covered in cowpats. It was this field across which I was chased by a ram, until I stumbled over and found it looking down at me with no great malevolence - and so the chase stopped. When, sometime later, in the same field, I spied a bull walking towards me from some distance, I did not wait for the closer chase, but as I walked away, in some doubt about reaching the stile to get out of the field, I began to hasten, and so did the bull. In the end, we were both at a fair gallop when I reached safety first.

Rogers's Lane was at our end of the village, and it led away from the main road in the direction opposite to the mill and brook. It then went up the hill at the back of our house, passed the crab apple trees near the haystacks at its brow, and alongside the next field for some distance, before it finally turned right towards Rogers's farm. We walked the lane often: we gathered wood to bring home for the fire, we picked blackberries in late summer and sloes in the depth of winter, we played in the haystacks, and, quite rarely, we went the whole way to Rogers's Farm, which was set in a dell surrounded by orchards and hawthorn hedges - isolated - and strange.

As smaller children, we sometimes walked up the lane with the older boy from next door who was blind, but could manage to follow along with us. He could not see the surrounding life as we could, but he was old enough to feel his own as it grew, and sometimes he shared these feelings with us. His sister was of our own age, and after we had played as mothers and fathers having tea in the safety of the huts in the corner of their field, it was she whom I first kissed by the haystack, and shared childhood feelings.

In the autumn, my foster brother Reg and I got as far as the orchard at the side of Rogers's farm when the apples were ripening on the trees. It was I who was induced to enter it and bring back an armful of what he declared were russets, and we both agreed were sour. We also reached there one quiet morning when the snow had just cleared from the fields, and there were bunches of snowdrops looking bright against the green grass alongside the orchard, and I knew that life was awakening again in our village countryside.

14

At the far corner where Rogers's Lane turned towards the farm we could leave it and cut diagonally across the field to the left to find the white mushrooms pushing through the dewy grass in the early autumn mornings. You could stoop between the cowpats and, with eager care, crook the first two fingers under the dome against the stem to extract them, complete, from the soil and grass, and take them home to her.

It was usually this way across the fields rather than through the village that we took to get to the Far Meadows where we built a den high in a willow tree, and made a wooden ladder to climb up to it. On the day when our ladder fell down and we were left up aloft, it was Reg who hung from a branch and then dropped, unhurt, on the grass below to rescue us, having declared that this was his duty as a Scout. The brook, where we met it again down there, smelt mossy, and was narrow enough to jump across, but I sometimes got a wet foot in doing so. In the village outside the pub one evening I fell completely into the brook, as I backed away from an argument with an adult, and got more than a wet foot.

At our end of the village, the houses, including the pub, were on our side of the road, and the brook ran alongside the other. It was crossed by one bridge, to reach the post office, and another, further down, to reach the little church, with its squat square tower, and Nixey's farm beyond, from which we fetched our milk. It was at this farm that we saw cart horses pull the great waggons on which the sheaves were piled after the wheat had been harvested, and we would be there later in the year when it was threshed, and would beat the escaping rats and mice with special hard hazel sticks.

Reg, the younger of her own two children, was my main companion for most of my four years in the village, for he was just a few months older than I. For a time we shared a double bed, and John, the older foster brother, shared with Jeff, in the other bedroom, but when the latter became fourteen and was returned to the Homes, the two real brothers shared, and we two younger ones from the Homes had the back bedroom. Often we lay there, awake, on summer evenings, and I gazed at the cracks in the plastered ceiling where the shape of a car could be made out.

My foster mother loved children easily and they loved her; those from the neighbouring houses would come in specially to see her, and always addressed her affectionately. On the occasions when the antics of four boys living in close proximity did not yield to her quiet remonstrations, she appealed to Dad who maintained authority by a thick leather belt, effective more by threat than usage. He was a big man and worked at the Pressed Steel factory in Oxford, some few miles away, when he was not being an officer's batman at the aerodrome. He sang in the church choir, but suffered a deafness attributed to the shells exploding around him in the trenches during the First World War, and as this disability increased, so did the length of time he spent in the local pub, and his ecclesiastical renditions became louder, and less reverent.

Having been born in that part of the country he had relatives in the nearby villages whom we visited after long country walks on Sundays. At home, he dug the back garden that went up the hill, and grew vegetables for us. At the top of the garden, he dug the pit into which he emptied the pail from the outside lavatory. He was an expert saw sharpener and for this had a large wooden frame and a collection of files and tooth benders; saws were brought from the neighbourhood and surrounding villages and with this, and the washing which Mum took in, they earned some extra money with which to keep their family of four. It was known in the village that we two boys came from the Homes, and it made no difference to our lives there.

Two parcels once arrived for my birthday and each contained a book sent by different people, both signing themselves as my mother. The arrangements by Barnardo's for children boarded out in foster homes included the forwarding of letters and gifts from relatives, but the addresses of the senders were withheld. So few clear memories of my first five years had come with me to the village that I could not explain why I had two other mothers, nor did I much mind, for my Mum was the little person there who loved and looked after me.

Another arrangement by the Homes included periodic inspections by an official visitor, who came unheralded, and usually had to find us at school in Watlington. We were taken out of our class to the cloakroom where we were weighed, measured, and generally assessed for our well-being. They would have had little to concern themselves with, for the hard work of our Mum and Dad kept all four of their children well fed and clothed, but we children from the Homes felt singled out by this inspection procedure.

The bus, which took us to school, was brown and quaintly broad in the beam - so was its driver, whom we called 'Colonel' Hicks. It took us and our paper bags of sandwiches to the spiky-roofed buildings in Watlington, which contained the classrooms where Miss Quarantine taught us our basic letters and numbers, and Miss Chapman read us Peter Pan and endless Enid Blyton Sunny Stories. It was the latter who got us to act and sing 'Good King Wenceslas', and when I was dressed in royal robes I noticed the long black hair of the girl alongside as I commanded: "hither page and stand by me".

The asphalt school playground had lime trees growing along one side, and a surrounding red brick wall. We could see over this well enough to watch the great twirling aeroplane as it fell to the ground across the other side of the road one day, and then burst into flames. Afterwards, the grown-ups said it was one of our own

Wellington bombers on the way back to Benson aerodrome that had crashed, and that they brought out the burnt and shrunken bodies of the crew on special stretchers, which got too hot to hold.

Other effects of the Second World War were felt, even in our little village. Gas masks and blackouts were part of our air raid precautions and it was held that it was some failure of the latter in one of our council houses one night that caused the cluster of bombs to be dropped over our heads and across the fields. The nearest one, in the hilltop just beyond our back garden, failed to explode, and we were able to view it, after it had been defused, at the bottom of a deep hole. Our near escape from the bombs may well have had more to do with Benson Aerodrome than our blackout failures, for we knew that this was a busy place during the Battle of Britain.

In addition to my foster Dad and others from the village, the aerodrome employed men from the big cities and it was one their families that was billeted on us and given one of our bedrooms, while we boys squeezed into the others. These lodgers brought the clothes and smells of the big cities with them, and were a source of extras, such as sweets, at a time when all luxuries and most of our food were rationed. I kissed the daughter of a lodging family one evening on our upstairs landing, so I suppose they also brought ways of life that appealed to us villagers.

It was the rationing, and the continued hardship in keeping four growing boys clothed and fed during wartime, that our Mum and Dad could no longer manage, and we boys from the Homes were sent back.

We were dispatched to a place known at that time as 'The Boys Garden City' at Woodford, on the East side of London. Among the motley crowd of children passing through Dr Barnardo's Homes in London during 1941, two little boys from a country village quite soon lost themselves - and each other. The Reception House, called Gordon Williams, was at the lower end of the 'Village

Home', and from there, during daytime, we looked across London at the barrage balloons shining silver in the sunlight above the city to protect it from the German bombers. At night, we could hear them coming over as we lay in our bunk beds, on or below the dining room tables; sometimes the throb of the planes was followed by the whine of a falling bomb and we awaited the explosion. Quite often, we could distinguish the crackling noise of the anti-aircraft fire. It was at bedtime that I most missed my foster Mum and I cried to myself. In the morning, all seemed quiet again and we saw no signs around us of bomb damage. Nevertheless, although we were some miles from the centre of the London blitz, most of The Boys Garden City had been evacuated to large country houses in East Anglia, and many cottages in the Village Home stood empty.

In the Reception House we fed and played under the watchful eyes of Mr and Mrs Cursey, a couple who maintained a strict regime amidst the comings, goings, and sorting out of a crowd of boys in a kind of transit camp. She wore a white dress uniform and a stiffly starched white hat with a great triangular flap behind it; she was short and rustled as she moved among us. We called her Matron, and she seemed very different from the little foster mother we had left behind. Matron's husband was less forbidding, but a little crusty, with a thin and slightly stooping figure clad in a sombre suit, sparse grey hair, and a brown-stained moustache. They looked after us while some kind of sorting occurred, for in a few days I was moved up the 'Village' to an adjacent cottage to await transferral out of London, to one of the country houses in East Anglia.

It was at this stage that I became separated from Terry, the other foster child, and I never saw him again.

The few weeks spent in this Barnardo transit camp, so near to London, were vividly impressive, and not only because of the nearby blitz, and the contrast with our little home in Oxfordshire. In the Village Home, I saw columns of boys with their heads shaven for the treatment of ringworm, and I watched a black boy having an epileptic fit beside the hot green corrugated tin building, which was our school - I saw the whites of his upturned eyes. I also met the skillful man with stumps for hands and watched him mend things in the little workshop beyond the school; it was said that he had spent all his life in Dr Barnardo's. I knew that I was with other homeless and unhappy boys, and we faced our plight together, and made companions during those few weeks.

I was nine years old when I was returned from my foster home to the institutional care of Dr Barnardo's, and I brought back with me the second part of my childhood. It had been formed amidst a family life in which love, beauty, and truth were simple and real, and it has served me well. During the next five years I wrote diligently to my foster mother who not only replied but also, when the state of the blitz over London, Barnardo's transport arrangements, and her own financial well-being permitted, provided me with a home for school holidays. My infrequent appearances in the village, wearing my Barnardo's institutional clothes, and, later, my Nautical School uniform, were increasingly as a stranger.

During one of those holidays, I had a fight with John Dix, previously one of my friends in the village, and I knocked him into the hawthorn hedge outside our house. On a later holiday, when some celebrations included a bonfire on the village green, I pursued self-promotion sufficiently to accept a dare to run along a log that lay across it. The log rolled as I was completing the challenge, and my knee was burnt, which was painful enough to me, but even more distressing to my foster Mum. However, while my institutionalised life progressively estranged me from my friends in the village, and from my foster brothers, it also deepened my affection for the person who had so loved me and for a while had provided me with a real home.

When I changed the uniformity of the Nautical School for the luxury of a public school, it was decided that my holidays would have to include the appropriate preparation of my clothes, personal possessions, and decorum for each ensuing term. They must have considered this to be beyond my foster mother's capability, and I began a long series of homeless holidays in different places - but I never forgot her.

I visited her while I was a student, and when I was training to become a doctor. In the years during which I travelled to England from various parts of the world, I came to see them all at Cuxham. Jeff, the older Barnardo boy, returned from the Navy and made his home there until he married, and he then made his own home and successful family life at nearby Princes Risborough. Reg, the foster brother who had been closest to me, also married, and left the home to make his own family life in Watlington. John almost married, but then remained with his parents as they grew to old age.

I last saw my foster father when he was in a hospital following a severe stroke, from which he did not recover. His speech was poor and his right side hardly moved, but he conveyed to me his pride in my progress since the time I had been their foster child; he said, inasmuch as he was able to, that I had done well.

She had always been frail, and in her later life had a major illness treated in the Radcliffe Infirmary at Oxford, during which time she was visited by a doctor who had been one of the two boys she had cared for during her time as a nanny. I saw her finally in the Nursing Home at Watlington, when she seemed even smaller, but the same gentle person, loved by all. That was shortly before the funeral in the Cuxham village church, where so many who had loved her were gathered, and her four grown boys amply filled the front pew. We said our prayers and then we easily bore her light coffin to the grave.

John remained at the home in Cuxham, and I saw him frequently throughout the following years while he diversified from farm worker to transport driver, and included motor mechanic, expert joiner, speedway driver, and dance band drummer in his many roles. When he died, from a mesothelioma of the lung contracted from one of his many occupations, the little church at Cuxham was again filled with friends and memories. We saw him join Ernest Arthur and Lily May Hook in the churchyard there, and Reg had the stone inscribed with their names. I have visited it since, with thoughtful gratitude, for there lies the happiest part of my childhood.

Popeye

"The lawns were dry in Euston Park,
Here truth inspires my tale,
The lonely footpath, still and dark,
Led over hill and dale."

This poem, entitled 'The Fakenham Ghost', is an account of a man followed on his way home across the parkland of Euston Hall to the nearby village of Fakenham by a pale spectre, against which he finally shuts his cottage door, only to discover a friendly sheep on the doorstep next morning. I knew the lines well when we lived there in the early 1940s, as Barnardo boys evacuated from the Boys Garden City in London. But the lawns were not dry in Euston Park, as we knew to our cost when we were marched up and down on them before breakfast by a stern lady called Miss Fernie, for our feet made patterns in the early morning dew, and our shoes got wet.

There were about sixty of us, of various shapes, colours, and sizes. The boys with deformities of their feet, or back, were called 'gammy', and a boy scarred over the shoulders, neck and face, was known as 'skellybug', while boys of Chinese or black parentage were known as 'chinky' and 'nigger' respectively. No disrespect was intended, for these were the means of identification that we used throughout Dr Barnardo's Homes, and they were part of the language of our institutionalised existence.

In charge was a Superintendent, who wore a blue sports jacket, which matched both his single real eye and the glass one on the other side, so that I always thought of him as a blue person; among ourselves, we called him 'Popeye'. Shortly after my arrival, he stopped me on my way up the staircase that led to that part of the Hall where we slept, and introduced me to another boy with the same unusual surname as mine. The other boy was thin and gentle-looking, with a humped back, and I did not know him, nor could I state whether or not we were related

23

since I knew so little of my earlier life, but I thought Popeye's gesture was friendly, and I was glad of it. It established a special but respectful relationship, which I retained throughout my time there; many other relationships were based upon awe, and sometimes fear.

Much of our life was centred on the corridor which led past our Dining Hall and out to the back yard. The Dining Hall had the hunting trophies of the past Dukes in the form of a great collection of animal heads on all the walls. On the side near the table at which I sat, the massive head of a buffalo was mounted just above that of a tiny mouse deer, which intrigued me. Over in the corner, just above the sink, was a boar's head, which must have lacked a few teeth, for it was the habit of the little stocky man who supervised our meals to place his smoking cigarette there. Our amusement was mixed with intimidation, for he always had with him a cane which swished as he struck it against his leather gaiters when walking along the flag-stoned corridor and across the floor of this great room, which, we were told, had been the Servants Hall. His surname was Carpenter, and we feared him, but called him 'Chippy' out of earshot.

Beyond the Dining Hall, the corridor turned left to the large double door, which opened into the back yard where we spent most of our playtimes. There we learnt the particular language with which we not only identified the nationality and physical deformities of our fellows, but also described our food, and the various authorities who looked after us, as though we had to couch some of the more important parts of our life in a code that was not shared by others.

The tin roof over the end of the yard adjacent to the back door had rows of holes in it and tales were told of how over-passing German bombers had machine-gunned the children. Perhaps they had other objectives, for outside the yard the Main Drive led to the right, past the side of the Hall, to the large Park around which there was

24

Things were better when I was promoted to the class round the corner. There we achieved such feats as reciting the whole of 'The Pied Piper of Hamlin' by heart, and we learned many other long poems. Sometimes we listened to the teacher, 'Professor' Joyce, reading endless tales of mud, motorbikes, and messengers in the Front Line of the First World War, when the yellow gas came up over the trenches. It was said that he had been there, and, with his wrinkled face, mustard-coloured moustache, and long hair, which gently shook as he coughed his way through these wartime tales, it all seemed very likely. It was also said that somewhere he had a cane, but never did he need to show it, for we held him in great awe.

The Headmaster was small, bald, and nicknamed Pip. His cane was as tall as he was, and fully visible where it stood outside his green-lined office somewhere between the downstairs corridor and the Duke's ballroom.

It was very infrequently that we saw the Duke or his staff, and only occasionally did we see the parts of the Hall in which he lived. Between our wing and Professor Joyce's classroom we passed a great stairway, and could overlook the carpeted space below that always seemed so quiet and deserted. The occasional concert by the troops, who sang the songs and told the jokes that sustained them during wartime, or an address from some important visitor, gained us access to the Ballroom, with its long windows lined by pink velvet curtains, and its shiny wooden floor. On certain wintry Sunday evenings the grey-haired matron with the glaring eyes somehow organised play sessions in which we sat around the periphery of this great room and handled special toys that we never saw at any other time. It was then that you noticed the two-holed electric sockets in the floor, covered by brass flaps, and the crystal glass chandeliers, but there were no pictures adding to the gilded decorations on the rich pink wall coverings.

We knew the Hall was E-shaped, reputedly because of its name, Euston, but perhaps a reflection of its Elizabethan origins, and the two open courts faced the Park, which was extensive, and lined by lime trees. There were clumps of trees dotted about it elsewhere, and these marked the boundaries of the area in which we played.

The open fronts of both courtyards could be viewed from the Park when we walked the path to the little church each Sunday to endure the ritual of morning and evening prayer as we sat, with our Matrons, filling the hard wooden pews. While those great rolling phrases and wonderful words entered our ears, to remain with us for ever, our eyes could watch the sun coming through the coloured glass of the windows, or follow the shape of the arches to the roof, and feel some kind of comfort from this distant God.

It was in the direction of the church that the Canary lay, behind quite a high flinted wall. Like areas of the Park beyond the clumps of trees, the Canary was out of bounds, but these limitations were happily, albeit carefully, broken when a very straight stick was needed to make an arrow suitable for a bow bent by string across a holly branch. Feathering the arrow seemed unnecessary when the distal end of the cane had a piece of wire around it, for this gave it weight such that it would fire quite straight, and also to a great height. The dangers of this past-time were never mentioned to us, but, oddly enough, the breaking of bounds in the Park, to gather and eat raw chestnuts from the distant trees, was said to be the reason why one of the boys was taken off to hospital to have an operation for acute appendicitis.

The soldiers' camp was also out of bounds, but we often talked to them during our playtime in the Park, and it was a friendly corporal who cut half-way round the ends of a large khaki petrol can for me, so that I could unfold it and use it as a kind of sledge to pull across the grass. My attachment to this as a possession, and a means to give rides to others, was considerable, for I fought with another boy who tried to take it from me and knocked him to the ground somewhere in the middle of the Park.

We were told not to board the back of the moving Army lorries, especially after a boy fell from one of them, and never recovered consciousness.

Among the more distant parts of the estate, which we rarely visited, was a part of the river Ouse, near a sluice gate, and this provided sufficient depth for swimming. We were taken there on very warm days when we were happy to discard all of our clothes and splash around quite naked. Even more important was the call for boys to go bracken pulling, and we went on farm vehicles to the other side of the estate where early crops were in competition with the weed as it uncurled through the soil surface. Our job was to walk along, straddling the rows, and stoop to break off the bracken shoots, for which we received some small payment. This was enough to treasure as the first money that I ever earned.

Despite the proximity of our army friends and the songs and jokes we heard at their entertainments, the war seemed distant, but our own immediate future in relation to it might well have entered into our talk with Popeye Lesley. He asked a group of us if we would like to join the Navy, and explained that Dr Barnardo's Homes included Watts Naval Training School, which trained boys for the Royal Navy, and Russell-Cotes Nautical School, which prepared them for the Merchant Navy. The latter was said to be less strict, and had more vacancies. We all would have preferred the former, and I particularly so, with the memory of the naval uniform from my early childhood, but it was to Russell-Cotes that three of us were sent.

Gussy Duck

When we three from Euston Hall were transferred to the Russell-Cotes Nautical School, at Parkstone, in Dorset, we took our Barnardo language with us: boys were mushes, new boys were new mushes, and the Matrons, who looked after us in the four houses which formed the residential part of the school, were called gussies. We were all put into the same house, named Arranmore, after the donor. Our Matron was Miss Drake who, with the apt intimacy of the Barnardo tongue, was known as Gussy Duck. Between her grey hair and double chin was a pale face with kind eyes that could twinkle, and we knew that beneath her firmness we had her affection.

In 1943, air raids directed on Poole Harbour were still occurring, and our iron-framed beds were crowded in the downstairs playroom as a precaution. When the reveille bugle called us out of our bunks she appeared, her ample frame covered by a faded green overall, and began to supervise our washing and dressing. We returned there each evening, after supper and supervised baths, to lie quietly while she put on the nine o'clock news for us to hear the latest from Winston Churchill, or the Front. Then came the Last Post bugle call which bade us pipe-down.

A life run by bugle calls had a welcome orderliness. We knew the tune of each off by heart, and many of them we set to words. The reveille, or 'Charlie', was cheerful, even on a cold dark winter morning. It began a routine of dressing, housework, and marching down to the mess deck, where hot pongy in aluminium bowls was covered by aluminium plates on which thick ginners of bread and melted marge were soft and warm. They were lined up on long, green-covered tables, where the boys fetched to early duty by the 'cooks to the galley' call had laid them. Mixed with the steaming tea in aluminium mugs, the smell was particular, and quite welcome to hungry boys.

A tall, elderly officer, who mostly stood at the end near the galley, supervised the Messdeck. When he moved across the wooden deck between the tables, he did so very slowly; we called him 'Stiffy'. His tongue, by contrast, moved fluently round the robust and colourful nautical language known to those who have served 'tween decks:

"I'll knock you through that bloody bulkhead!"

"You're neither use nor ornament!"

"Ye Gods and little fishes!" he would say.

It was a tirade sufficient to control some hundred and fifty boys, and I never knew him keep his threats of physical violence. When he took off his officer's cap you noticed his thick curly grey hair, and his shrewd old blue eyes softened a little one day at the boot inspection as I showed him yet another pair which I had worn-out from hard playing and marching on the parade ground.

This parade ground was the centre of our nautical life, for here, we learnt to march back and forth in the PT lessons, to salute, to keep time with the band, and on Sundays to line up for inspection and Church parade. Here also we spent hours of playtime quite happily, with the odd tennis ball, a few stones, or a piece of chalk to help us.

The Nautical School was built on the side of a hill, which continued above it to become a sandy cliff surmounted by Carter's Tower, overlooking Poole Harbour. The cliff and the wooded area immediately below it were strictly out of bounds, but only a thin hedge separated them from the Top Field, where we spent evening and weekend playtimes in the summer. It was possible to slip through this hedge, when the officer on duty was out of sight, and to creep among the pine trees to smell the resin, and to watch the large ants crawling along the sand on those hot sunny afternoons. The officer usually on duty during the playtimes was a short stocky man with a small amount of dark hair below the cap which he only occasionally took off. We called him Tubby. He said very little, but had good command of the boys, and a soft side to him. One day I squatted quite still among the bushes below the pine trees when I saw him coming into the woods there; he came close, and appeared to look directly towards where I crouched, but he said nothing - nor did I. Ever afterwards, I was sure that he had seen me out of bounds, but had let me off.

The four houses in which we lived were on a bank arranged in a quadrant above the parade ground; the three on the right, Arranmore, Howard and Johnson, housed all the boys below fourteen years of age, and we were called 'elementaries' because we had not yet left school to become committed to full daytime training for going to sea. Those who had were called 'nauticals' and lived in Broughton House, on the left. All boys wore dark blue naval uniform and pill-box cap, but the elementaries had a simple jersey and shorts, while the nauticals wore the full naval collar, lanyard, and long trousers, enlarged towards the feet, and known as 'bell-bottoms'. Each boy folded and kept his uniform clean and daily polished his boots; we kept our shoes for the Sunday parade, and for Saturday afternoon leave into the town.

Below and to the right of our house was the chapel, separated from the parade ground by a bank of brick tiles that became warm from the facing sun throughout the day. We sat for many an hour against this warm bank playing fivestones, or just talking to friends. The chapel was built of brick, in rectangular form, with long windows in the side facing the sun, but no arches. Gussy Duck replaced her green overall with more formal clothes to play the organ there for the Sunday Service, and we in the choir learnt to sing hymns lustily to her accompaniment. The music which she played before and after the service became familiar tunes to which we could set words of our own, and from the choir pews we watched her plump figure with some affection and familiarity as it swayed to each side on the small organ stool. It was from respect for her that I joined the confirmation class and one Sunday knelt reverently at the altar rail and made promises before a bishop, which were serious commitments, and he laid his hands on my head. It was also for her that I continued to sing in the choir when my voice no longer easily reached the top notes.

Among the visiting preachers, there was one of such stature that, as he leaned forwards from the pulpit in his grey suit with long lapels, he towered impressively over his young congregation while he declared:

" Trust in the Lord with all thy heart, and lean not under thine own understanding,

In all thy ways acknowledge Him and He will direct thy path."

We called him 'Bulldog', either from his size, or from the manner in which he worried the meaning out of his texts. That particular one remained with me and I resorted to it at those moments of decision when I could not clearly see what lay ahead.

The bugle called us not only to the cookhouse door, but also to assemble for morning parade and prayers, for school, for playtime breaks, and for the practice sessions of the band and the gymnastics team. This ordered life, the strict discipline enforced by cane or cuff, and the nautical language used for its events and surroundings, came easily enough to me. Good conduct was rewarded with weekly points which accumulated towards a red, then silver, then gold star badge which, when earned, was worn on the arm of the uniform. It was possible, with some diligence, to get to the gold star stage while still an elementary, between the ages of ten and fourteen, and the achievement carried with it a similarly graded increase in the fortnightly pocket money. We saved some of this in a kind of nest-egg account for large items, and the rest we spent in town on a Saturday afternoon. This form of prowess by good conduct was different from that determined by the physical ability to march or run a long distance in the heat or cold, to play cricket or football on the Top or Bottom Field, do gymnastics, endure a beating, and, ultimately, to maintain a position in relationship to the other boys by fighting them, if necessary. We either met the challenge to fight, surrounded by onlookers, until the outcome was clear, or refused it, with a loss of standing.

To the right of the parade ground a roadway led past the woodwork room, beyond which was another illicit entry to the pinewoods, and the road thereafter went uphill to the Sickbay and the swimming pool. On the way up, in a wooden hut on the right, was the Seamanship Room. In my third year, I was given this as a special duty to attend to between breakfast and school time, when most of the other elementaries were cleaning and tidying their own house. My job was to sweep, dust and tidy this room, which was easy enough, and I spent most of my time polishing the brass of the compass binnacle and the attached helm, or figuring out the complex knots in the tarred ropes, or looking at the flags, anchors and other nautical objects there. Seamanship classes were part of the schooling, even for the elementaries, and it was not difficult to learn to box the compass, signal by semaphore or Morse code, read the great flags of the International Code of Signals, tie knots - some useful and some decorative - and recite the doggerel poems that enshrined the Rules of the Road for Vessels at Sea. They also taught us the meaning of the various marking buoys, how to read a navigation chart, and how to sound depths with a lead line - all acquisitions in anticipation of becoming a nautical in due course. To me, the smell of tar and brasso, which I met each early morning in the Seamanship Room, was part of the life at sea for which I was bound.

The majority of the elementaries were increasingly set on going to sea, and the tales of the older boys, who returned to visit us at the school after being aboard for a while, were so full of the ports and docksides they had seen, and the life on the ocean, that they made us more so.

Marking time before becoming a nautical was helped by the band and the gymnastics team, for both included elementaries, and for the one I learnt to play the fife, and the other to do somersaults, handstands, and various feats acquired with a little agility - and a lot of practice. In both of these pursuits I shared a friendship with Colin Leaney, who was naturally musical and agile, and at those times when we were able to take out our fifes for practice, he taught me to play a song about a trout, and tunes other than the marches which we were supposedly practising. He seemed to have come to the nautical school from a family home rather than from another Barnardo's institution, and, although able to do the gymnastics with encouragement, was not naval by inclination; it was always clear that he would not stay to become a nautical. We became good friends, and it was friendships that gave warmth and comfort to our lives.

The band and gym team, either separately or together, made outings to entertain the surrounding community at garden fetes, factory canteens, and special parades in the town, such as those on Empire Sunday. We not only learnt how to perform in public, but also how to meet people outside our own institution. In addition, our involvement brought us further badges and increases in our pocket money.

Assistant matrons came and went in Arranmore House, with only slight passing effect on us. However, the system whereby each house had one of the nauticals as a Petty Officer, and one of the elementaries as a Leading Hand (known as a Leader), affected us profoundly. It was the duty of these two to maintain the moment-to-moment discipline by firm word of command, shouting, or by frank physical assault, depending upon their natural authority and physical status among the boys whom they supervised. The Leader had the advantage of belonging to the house, as an elementary who had been promoted from among the others by the Matron, whereas the Petty Officer had come from the nautical house and was imposed upon the elementaries by the authority of the Commanding Officer. When I first became a Leader, appointed by Gussy Duck, I was glad to have a Petty Officer who was a friend such that our relationship became intimate, and I not only permitted this, but took some comfort from it. Some boys found neither support nor friendship within this strict system, and incurred punishments which ranged from restrictions of privileges to strikes of the cane - 'six of the best". In their restiveness they would sometimes 'do a bunk', only to be brought back after a day or two, with tales of how they had managed in the outside world before being found by the police; their notoriety for a few weeks brought them attention and comfort of a sort.

The more accepted means of seeing the world outside were the ceremonial occasions down in Poole, with the band in the lead, or on the Sunday afternoon walks, conducted in four abreast columns (but not in marching step), and the outings with the gymnastics team or band. There was also an afternoon leave granted every other Saturday, when full uniform would be donned, and with a friend of your own choice, and a little of your pocket money, you could go down to the town for small shopping, or for a paddle-boat trip on the lake in the park. The town lay somewhat lower than the school, between it and Poole Harbour, where the nauticals did their practical seamanship on board the small boats. The part of the town across the railway was out of bounds, but this never precluded me from visiting the museum, only a short distance beyond, for it had a fascinating collection of stuffed animals, insects, and butterflies. One of the last was arranged in the form of a large compass, with all its points, which always intrigued me. Being the museum of a town with a harbour and visiting ships, there was a nautical atmosphere within which somehow served to justify this breaking of bounds.

We had some kind of choice over our visits to the photographer in town, for although these were official, and attended in full uniform, one could go with a friend, and even be photographed with him if so desired. Doubtless one of the prints joined those assembled for the records kept by Dr Barnardo's Homes, but the others were our own, and from among our few treasured possessions could be given to friends, or swapped for other items. A few boys had relatives or friends to whom to send them, and I sent one of mine to my foster-parents. I put a collection of these photographs from other boys, which I had, into a small album that I bought with my own money. Whenever I looked through it, I would recall each boy by his surname and number, as indeed officers, house-matrons, and teachers addressed us. There were only a few very close friends whom I knew by first name.

Each boy had a locker for his personal possessions along a wall of the downstairs playroom, and it was there that we kept our individual lives. I had the letters from my foster mother, my collection of foreign stamps, my book of friends' photographs, the toy car that I had brought back from Cuxham, and a book into which I pasted pictures of buildings, such as New York's skyscrapers and Sydney Harbour Bridge. By some unwritten but powerful rule, boys did not steal from each other's lockers.

Good people who lived in Parkstone, Poole, or Bournemouth 'adopted' certain individual boys as weekend visitors, and provided them with a meal, or a visit to the cinema, but we always wore our uniform on these forays to the outside world.

In 1945, at the beginning of my fourth year at Russell-Cotes, my friendly Petty Officer went off to sea. I liked his successor well, but knew that he favoured one of my friends. These friendships were often expressed by having our photographs taken as pairs, and I counted them as special additions to my collection. It has remained with me as a vivid record of our feelings and values at that time, for it was around then that Gussy Duck retired, and things changed.

Pop Bailey

"Where are those bricks there?" he would shout, referring to the wall ahead of us. We were supposed to look at it and fix on a brick. He was Mr Dayley, the headmaster with the bristling moustache, and he liked to parade us before school. His favourite exclamation was "Carrambah" and he was reputedly Irish. Not all of the schoolteachers were so martial, but our formal schooling was much coloured by the nautical training, and less by the local education authority. In my first two years, placement in the classes was determined by ability, and it proved possible to work from the bottom to the top.

Two of the classrooms were at a lower level than the parade ground, in a green-painted wooden building beside the platform on which was the lifeboat used for practicing the raising and lowering of boats at sea. In one of these classrooms, 'Buck' Newton maintained authority by his ability to cock his long tweed-clad leg over a boy's head, but he did not use a cane. The teacher in the adjacent class was a dark and dapper man with a little black moustache.

The next class up was on the second floor of the Lady Russell-Cotes House - the building on the south side of the parade ground, with not only bricks to be fixed upon, but also with the Headmaster's Office, and the Commanding Officer's Boardroom. As befitted the bridge of our ship, it was also the domain of the Officer of the Watch, complete with quartermaster's desk, and a Bell Boy who struck the appropriate number for each watch, as in a vessel at sea.

We called the teacher of the third class 'Pi' by a useful contraction of his name - Pionchin. He was small and somewhat crabbed, like his writing on the blackboard, and smiled only occasionally. As I stood beside his desk while he went over my work, I could read, from the name on the badge in his lapel, that he was an "Old

Contemptible" and I associated this with his method of teaching by writing lots of dates and facts on the blackboard in close style, and expecting us to learn them. He was tired-looking, but diligent, and he had a thick and knobbly brown cane, which he occasionally used. Withal, we respected him, and worked hard.

The teacher of the top class was known as 'Pop' Bailey, although he was only mildly rotund, and the appellation was more one of respectful affection. He was a particularly thoughtful person who wore a chocolate-coloured striped suit, and had thick-rimmed spectacles through which his grey-blue eyes looked shrewdly, but kindly. He gave us individual attention and knew us well for what we were. Ken Richmond, a boy some few months older than I, was at the top of Pop Bailey's class when I reached it, and we became competitors for first place in the examinations. Pop oversaw this rivalry with great fairness.

Inasmuch as some of our lessons in the elementary class were on seamanship, it was also necessary for the nauticals to continue their general education, and masters for the lessons were switched so that we had Mr Crisp from the nautical class upstairs. He wore a blue jacket, and had a fringe of white hair around his bald head; he had served long in India. The lessons with him always had an air of travel and the British Empire, with tales of Poona and the Black Hole of Calcutta, the poems of Newbolt and Kipling, and stories of Gurkhas, Sikhs and snakes.

The Lady Russell-Cotes House also contained the school library. It had glass-fronted bookcases around the walls and a big table in the middle at which I sat for many an hour reading Percy F Westerman's adventure stories, tales of foreign lands by G A Henty, or Captain W E John's accounts of Biggles in the Air Force, which was topical enough. Our other reading tastes were influenced by the remarkable collection of volumes of Punch and the

London Illustrated News which were scattered around on the tables in the Dining Hall to occupy us on those wet week-end afternoons when we could not be out on the parade ground. Hours spent turning the pages of these great tomes impressed upon me the buildings and state occasions of London, and the word Charavari for English satire, and left me with an affection for the smell of those old books, and the feel of the pages with the fine engravings that constituted the illustrations.

Nor did we lack reference books, for I wrote at least two essays for the annual competitions run by the British Empire Society, and remember poring over the chapters on the island known then as Ceylon, and the description of the reputedly godly footprint on the mountainside of Adam's Peak. Two books of poetry were the prize I obtained, in 1946, for the best essay on "The Empire as the Source of the Nation's Food Supply" - the subject of the prize has proved longer lasting than that of the essay. Barnardo's, our nautical training, and the British Empire, were all features of RCNS that were bound to have made their mark on me, but my interests in poetry, and in the famous buildings that I pasted in my scrapbook, were different; they stemmed from our schoolteachers such as Pop Bailey and Mr Crisp.

The change in my response to authority at Russell-Cotes began when I was aged thirteen. Our elderly and friendly Matron left, and was replaced by a new one who was quite young, glared at us whenever exerting her authority, and colluded with a heavy-handed Petty Officer. One day, I thought she had treated us unfairly in deciding that we had not properly polished the dormitory floor; she had ordered us to return during our afternoon playtime to repeat the task. The team of boys was under my charge as the Leader. I brought them back, and arranged only to move the beds and sweep the room, but not to polish it. She inspected and passed it as much better. I then told her that we had not actually polished it any further. For this challenge to her authority, I was placed before the Commanding Officer at the Morning Assembly on the Messdeck. I had by then been a Leader for some time, and had a gold star good conduct badge, as well as being a fife-player in the band, and one of the few elementaries in the gymnastics team. The Skipper, an aloof person with a manner of drawling his commands that induced ridicule rather than respect, reprimanded, but did not demote or otherwise punish me. It could have been worse, for it was at this Morning Assembly on the Mess Deck, that he would punish boys who had committed major offences by 'six of the best'. In the presence of the whole school, officers, and house Matrons he administered these across the bent-over bottom of the boy with a long pliant cane, which swished with each stroke. He would then turn to the lectern to give the Bible reading and prayers for the day.

It was a measure of the goodness of my foster parents and the consideration shown by Barnardo's that during those wartime summer holidays I was one of those able to go on 'home leave', to use the nautical term. In 1945 however, the doodlebugs and rockets falling without warning on major cities precluded such journeys, and we were sent to camp in the grounds of Canford School. We pitched our tents on one side of the main buildings, and the river Stour was on the other. I remember seeing some of the boys from the public school, who must have come back early for their term, and I heard the polished manner in which they spoke and behaved.

The camp was greatly enjoyed, for we were allowed to swim in the river, indeed, could dive off the top of the wheel which controlled the lock-gates, if the officer was not looking, and we could also walk down into the nearby village without accompanying staff. It was there that four of us climbed over a wall into an orchard and stole some apples. We were seen by a villager, who reported us to the Chief Officer. He assembled the camp and we were all identified and brought before him. Three of us acknowledged our crime, and he gave us six strokes of the cane across our bottoms. The fourth member of the gang denied all, and he was given only four of the best. No one cried at the time, but I went back to my tent and sobbed miserably, not because of the punishment I had received, but because of the reduction in that of the boy who had lied. It began a dislike of the Chief Officer who had made the arbitrary decision, and I retained this thereafter, although I knew him to be quite a considerate person, particularly to the more successful boys among the nauticals.

Changes in the school education arrangements also occurred at this stage; a new headmaster appeared and re-organised the classes by age. He threatened me with a move downwards, but Pop Bailey defended my position, and I remained at the top of his class. Perhaps all of this had some part in the conversation that I overheard while waiting outside the Boardroom one morning. The Skipper was talking to the new headmaster, an angular and articulate man who had replaced Carrambah Dayley. Pop Bailey also was there, and they were considering two of us for a place in another school. It was apparent that Pop had to defend my inclusion in this opportunity, and put my position as first in the class against some disaffection shown by the other two. He was again successful, for both Ken Richmond and I were sent to London for the final selection. Much must have depended upon our presentation and performance there. Perhaps the fact that he was some months older than I mattered for, although I had gained the lead in the class examination results, he had a longer-standing good conduct record, and, like I, had been a Leader in his own house, and a member of the band and gym team. At the time we went to London he was well on the way to becoming a successful nautical.

The opportunity, which was finally given to me, was that of a place in a public school. The privilege of this was so great that neither I nor anyone else considered the abandonment of the life at sea, to which I had given my heart and soul for some few years. Pop Bailey had supported me, and I respected his opinion that this was the right step for me to take.

The class work had already become repetitive, and he not only provided me with extra tuition in maths, but also encouraged my reading, and gave me the interesting chance to work on the typewriter in his office, and to write formal letters. Elsewhere in the school, I was seen as someone especially marked out for a different life, and this made my last few months there somewhat uncomfortable, particularly with the Chief Officer.

The summer holidays that year were also very different, for I spent them at 18-26 Stepney Causeway, the Barnardo Headquarters in East London. There I was being prepared for a place at Bryanston School, and this was done by employing me as the Messenger Boy for the Headquarter Offices, when I was not being taken to the 'Gifts in Kind' Department at Barkingside to be fitted with items of clothing which matched the more ordinary ones on a long School List. I was taken to Gorringes, the great shop in Central London, for the items exclusive to the school.

Barnardo's met the school requirements in a manner that had late repercussions, for some items from the 'Gifts in Kind' Department at Barkingside were distinctly quaint. The maroon sweater and brown corduroy shorts which I sported at weekends and free afternoons were particularly individual, but, being my first non-uniform items of clothing for many years, they became my favourites. I had a quite unconventional tuckbox, and my school trunk was a massive brassbound affair which, to judge from its many labels, had already travelled the world, and was more than second-hand.

44

When filled to the top, it taxed the abilities of two hefty railway porters to move it. My neat blue suit, with long trousers, had the label of Gorringes, London, on the inside, and I knew that, in this important respect, I was conventionally equipped for Bryanston.

My daytime role of delivering letters and messages around the honeycomb of offices that, in 1946, constituted the Headquarters of Dr Barnardo's Homes at 18-26 Stepney Causeway, in East London, not only encouraged some ability in orientation, but also induced me to address the various staff members with the necessary courtesy, and to become acquainted with the roles and status of a number of them. Nor did the historical significance of those buildings escape me, for down in the Entrance Hall, from whence I collected the daily mail, there stood against the wall, alongside the Commissioner's Office, the 'Ever Open Door' of Dr Barnardo's original Reception House in Stepney.

In 1946, only a few boys actually lived at the Headquarters; a house where Stepney Causeway adjoined the Commercial Road was run as a hostel for boys in transit. Mr and Mrs Cursey, the couple who had the care of Gordon Williams House in the Boys Garden City at the time of my return to Barnardo's from Oxfordshire, were by then at Stepney. I found them comfortingly familiar, and by no means so severe, after my four years at Russell-Cotes.

My evening times and weekends were spent wandering around East London. I came to know the buildings of Commercial Road in detail, and I walked in the direction of the London Docks, and found the green park on the edge of the Thames where you could enter the stairway around the ventilation shafts of the Rotherhithe Tunnel. I went down there one day, past the great whirring fans, into the tunnel alongside the roaring traffic, and I walked under the Thames to the other side.

On these long walks I was alone, with my own thoughts and feelings, and kept myself so; I was never in any way accosted, and I developed a personal knowledge of the East London which Barnardo had trod, looking for homeless children. Furthermore, I became acquainted with the staff at the Barnardo Headquarters sufficiently to know who such as Miss Carlyle, Miss Chavasse, Mr Bazalgette, the Reverend Snowden-Smith, and Mr Lucette were - two of them later became important adults to me.

When I went to Bryanston, I remembered Pop Bailey's support and encouragement at Russell-Cotes, and held as important the premise that I had been given an opportunity that was rare for a Barnardo boy. Occasionally, I wrote to him, and he knew that some good came of my time at a public school. Later, I had the privilege of visiting him and his wife at their home after his retirement, and thereby expressed in some way my gratitude to him. When I wrote to her after his death, she replied that he had been proud of me; I knew that he had cared enough to teach and support me beyond the ordinary.

Joyce Wilson

From my position on the outskirts of the crowd around the notice board, I could see nothing, and it began to seem hopeless. The boys in front talked in voices with a pitch and intonation to which I was unaccustomed, and pronounced their extensive English vocabulary and phrases in a fashion to which I was a stranger, and I felt alone and unhappy. Most of them were new boys but, unlike me, they had been to traditional preparatory schools where they had already been taught Latin and French, and had sat the Common Entrance Examination. I had no knowledge of languages other than basic English, and had sat only the Bursary Examination for which I had visited the school a month or two earlier, dressed in my nautical uniform. Bryanston, in its huge red-brick building faced with Portland stone, was awesome enough to any prospective pupil, and a bursary boy from Barnardo's had reason to know his shortcomings.

The English 'public' schools gained their name from the distant times when they ceased to be primarily religious foundations and opened their doors to members of the public - for a fee. The progressive increase of the fee-paying component produced institutions virtually exclusive to the upper classes in the 18th and 19th centuries, and to the moneyed classes in the 20th. Despite their name, they were private institutions, although most retained a few places for the financially less well endowed, based on scholarship. Bryanston, founded in 1927, with the motto *'et nova et vetera'* aimed to include the best of the new and the old in a boarding public school. Its educational methods, modified from the Dalton system, gave pupils much freedom of choice, and attracted entrants with artistic and freethinking backgrounds. Its admissions policy, by the 1940's, included boys from a variety of social backgrounds, with quite a few places being re-imbursed by various industries, local education

47

authorities, and organisations, but the inclusion of Barnardo's among these was by some very particular arrangement, to which I was never fully a part.

To the percipient, these 'bursary' boys were distinguishable by their speech and limited educational background at the time of their admission, but the equality of opportunity which Bryanston provided soon made individual achievement the determinant of relationships; origins and background were irrelevant and not much discussed.

This equality of opportunity and freedom of choice in the system entailed a complex timetable; it also required that every pupil should have a personal tutor to steer his choices between the extremes of artistic endeavour expressed by some parents, and the conventional academic demands made by others. The appointment of a tutor to the individual new boys with bursary positions, and without strong parental preferences, might well have been in the lap of the gods, but I suspect one godly man whom I came to admire had a hand in it. Who else would have put a conscientious, over-disciplined, parentless fourteen-year-old in the care of a teacher with the distinctions, relatively rare at that time, of being a woman graduate in Chemistry from Oxford, and the Head of Science in a boys public school; who made-up her face and nails colourfully, exuded perfume, dressed her well-curved figure in the best fashionable clothes, and conveyed it to and from the school in a large car, driven always with aplomb?

Her room, where I first found her soon after my arrival at the school, was at the top of the long spiral stone stairway beside the main entrance to the school building. She sat with her legs curled sideways on a large sofa and, with a disarming smile, explained the complicated system. My lack of previous education should have put me in the lowest year, but my age was more suitable for the next one up, with two years to go for the School Certificate. My

48

credentials had me placed in the lowest 'sets' for most subjects, but a little higher for Maths, and I was also put down for music lessons on the piano and flute, for reasons which were never clear to me.

In each week certain lessons were at fixed times, and between these were free periods in which assigned work for each subject was done. The choice as to which lot of assigned work I did, and at what time, was mine, as was the use of the evening prep periods, but all was to be entered in the monthly chart kept by each pupil. On the back was entered how each period of the day was spent, and the number of periods used for each subject was entered on the front, beneath the box in which the subject teacher entered the weekly marks. An honestly kept chart reflected the time and commitment given to each subject - a 'cooked' chart resulted from a lack of diligence, or a poor memory, and had a conventional conformity which deceived few tutors.

From this first encounter with Joyce Wilson I took away more of her womanly presence than her explanation of the system, but I knew that I must see the big timetable on the notice board in the Main Hall, in order to know whether or not one of my sets had a class, and in which classroom it was to be held. I was also carrying with me enough books, folders, and paper to cope with either an assignment period or class, and I had with me an old-fashioned dip pen and ink. Struggling at the edge of the crowd, it was most particularly the clutching of the bottle of ink that added to my estrangement, and in my distress, I turned to the nearby staircase to seek her help. It was a long way to her room at the top, and I was still tearful when I reached her and explained some of my difficulties. She listened with a charming smile, and gave me a fountain pen.

During the following four years, I climbed that stairway at least weekly, and sometimes more often, as I presented my chart, or my problem, for perusal and discussion by her, with always encouragement and a smiling persuasiveness that brought from me endeavour, and acceptance. It was a relationship of respect for academic progression, and never again did personal emotions obtrude, but I always knew that I had a good tutor.

The 'nova' of Bryanston's aspirations included no fagging by juniors for seniors, no punishment by beatings, an informal uniform of grey-blue shirts and shorts, and the convention of calling the school years Blocks D to A respectively; the forms (or classes) of other public schools were actually called 'sets', and were decided entirely by ability. In the first year, in block C, I was moved up a set or so each term, for some natural ability in Maths eased my way through the science subjects, and a real enjoyment of English and History helped me through the arts. The problem of having learnt no French beforehand was solved by making German my foreign language, and I joined a special set created for beginners. The examinations at the end of the first year must have justified my tutor's confident smile, for I was placed in the top sets for the next and all-important School Certificate year. In this renowned measure of our education, I managed a collection of credits and distinctions across both sciences and arts. Although I was more able at the former, I found the latter more enjoyable, and I did not view myself as a natural scientist; I was attracted to other people and already influenced by personal relationships, and ideas.

It was my tutor who suggested that I should aim for medicine, and I began my third year at the school with the appropriate mixture of subjects for that direction. She also thought that I should aim for one of the older universities, which required some knowledge of Latin for entrance. 'Tigger' (TG) Hoare, who mainly directed physical education in the school, and played the fiddle for the Country Dancing Club, taught this to a specially constructed small class. His Latin had an ecclesiastical flavour, but he imparted sufficient for me to pass the Cambridge University Entrance Examination called "Little Go", and to retain thereafter some appreciation of etymology.

Unlike Barnardo's, and many traditional public schools, Bryanston did not have a slang language, and there was almost an aversion to using the conventional school expressions common at that time. Teachers were occasionally referred to by their forenames, or nicknames, but more commonly known by their initials, while prefects, monitors, other boys, games, tuckshop, and chapel were all known as such.

In my first two years, I was more impressed by the teachers of subjects other than Science. Wilf Cowley, who taught English, expected us to read original Chaucer text aloud in class, with suitable expression, and when a boy called Michael Rodd expressed his distaste for this, he dryly quipped:

> "*How odd*
> *That Rodd*
> *Should refuse*
> *To amuse*"

He taught us to make an anthology of the poetry which we liked, and when writing an essay, to make a big heap of ideas, and then to sort these in smaller piles, like with like. In addition to The Prologue and Nun's Priest's Tale, we studied Eliza Doolittle and Professor Higgins, and the desertion and murder of Julius Caesar by his friends. Long after I had departed from the ranks of those primarily studying English, on one particular March 15th, when I was the duty monitor at the Dining Room door with the task of vetting latecomers, he wrote a chit to accompany a boy which read: "Detained by me, WSHC, The Ides of March". His wit was as penetrating as his teaching of English, and the twinkle of his blue eyes made my distant affection greater than my fear of him. I became a member of the Library Committee under his chairmanship, responsible, among other matters, for reviewing recently published books. From the latest acquisitions of the library I reviewed one which described how green was a Welsh valley, and another about Brighton in which a woman with nails painted as boldly as my tutor's, gestured with her 'red beetles'. My reviews were duly posted in the library, and I was glad enough to know they had his approval.

The Bryanston ideas in education were already spreading, and a girls' school with a similar system was started nearby, at Cranbourne Chase, but known to us as Crichel. We were joined by Crichel girls for the performance of plays, orchestral and choral concerts, the activities of the various school cultural societies, for social occasions such as dances, and for some of the more specialised classes, including a few in the sciences. Among the visiting girls, I found a dark-haired one with fine eyes distinctly attractive, most especially when I learnt that she was Wilf Cowley's daughter. I met the cheerful kindness of his wife at the Christmas pantomime one year, when Wilf Cowley combined with his colleague in the English department, Eric Brammell, to become the 'Babes in the Wood'. She was the helpful wardrobe mistress, back-stage, when I was struggling with some rapid costume changes.

Reading beyond the necessities of school studies became a private consolation to me, and, while I may well have started with Aldous Huxley as a writer with a known background in science, and followed him through "Brave New World', I was soon caught by his overall penetration and fluency. I was deeply impressed by reading of the effect of Bach's Mass in B minor in his essay 'Music at Night' and went on to read of the dramatic presentation of tragedy centred on the knock of the night watchman in

Macbeth, and others of his essays. It was then easy to read 'Grey Eminence' and to become aware of the great dialectic of the spiritual and political. 'Chrome Yellow' and 'Eyeless in Gaza' had impressed me well before I learnt of his own personal experience of failing vision, and hallucinogenic drugs. Thus, the initial scientific bent of my literary taste changed and I soon became involved in the intensely personal entanglements of Dostoevsky's writing, which I followed with a period of devotion to other Russian writers. In this way, a more personal interest replaced those that I had easily shared with other boys studying science, some of whom were involved in editing the school magazine, 'The Bryanston Saga', and later became professional writers.

I was taught English History by Harold Greenleaves, a master whom we respected for his physical and intellectual discipline. His attendance on the rugby field sporting a blazer of the Oxford and Cambridge Rugby Union Football Club ('The Greyhounds') somehow imbued in me respect for the English Industrial Revolution. When I learnt that he practised the visual exercises described by Bates in "The Art of Seeing" -the book which had so greatly influenced Aldous Huxley - I knew why he quite regularly placed his palms over his eyes as he sat in his chair at the end of the History Room in which we were all quietly working away at our assignments. By contrast, J C Royds, the teacher of American History, was a flamboyant person who sketched the characters of some of the American presidents so vividly that they remained with me forever ("get behind me Mr van Buren" said one of them to his vice-president when threatened by an assassin). He also had my respect for the skill with which he bowled slow googlies and coached the first cricket eleven to a standard of excellence. It was my ambition to meet his standards and be chosen for the team, but on the day that occurred, I was already occupying a regular place in the school athletics squad, and the matches coincided; somehow, I managed to appear for both events, but it was the cricket master's disfavour that I earned, and he never chose me again.

Specialisation in my last two years, however, meant that I spent much of my time with the teachers in the science department. The more advanced Chemistry taught by Joyce Wilson, my tutor, came easily enough since she used a university method of teaching. Physics, as presented by a young master, Teddy Potter, newer to the school than I, was not too difficult to comprehend, but Biology was the most enjoyable of them all. For some of us it was to lead to higher examinations in both Botany and Zoology, and Dick Harthan, our teacher of these, had great diligence and patience. During one class, I had my head in a book from the library, which I was reading below the desk, and did not notice he was behind me until too late. He gently acknowledged my interest in the non-biological subject of the book, and discussed it with the whole class; I never behaved badly for him again, and from his teaching not only acquired enough of zoology to pass the examination and approach medicine with some confidence, but also, from the botany, gained a life-long enjoyment of plants.

The array of societies and clubs for the pursuit of hobbies at the school was bewildering to a newcomer previously contented with collecting pictures of buildings and uniform photographs of his companions in Dr Barnardo's Homes. Model Railways and Natural History seemed to require a degree of previous acquaintance, but among the arts and crafts were places for beginners, and I spent a term or two hammering at alabaster with a chisel as I felt for a shape, guided by the hands of Don Potter, who was a stockily built sculptor with long hair. He had trained under Eric Gill, and was an unconventional teacher in a not very conventional public school.

Then I discovered the Printing Club, which had a proper apprenticeship, and a good collection of type fonts.

I began as a Novice, and progressed to Journeyman Printer, as I learned to be a compositor of notices and programmes that we printed for the school. The type was selected from wooden trays, designed with respect for the frequency and use of each letter, and among the faces the Gill Sans Serif became my favourite. In due course, I supervised the performance of the great hand press with which we printed our compositions, and when I had taken the responsibility for the total design and execution of a specific piece of work, I became a Master Printer. The whole experience of an apprenticeship not only taught me a craft, now long displaced, but also the processes necessary for acquiring a particular skill and working with other people.

It was a feature of the school that all pupils spent one of their afternoon sports periods doing some kind of useful work around the school, termed pioneering, and my bell maintenance job met this requirement. The task of maintaining the school bell system required no better qualification than sharing a study with a boy well on his way to obtaining an open scholarship in Physics at Cambridge, for it was Adrian March who was the expert in electricity behind the system, and I was his assistant.

He also had the skill to put together his own record-player on which he played overtures and selections of operas derived from his holiday-time spent with his parents in Vienna; quite often the Pilgrims' Chorus from Tannhauser could be heard well across the great courtyard of the school. These expressions of his musical taste were an effective antidote to the disparagement of Richard Wagner by then prevalent among our music mentors.

It was Adrian's expertise that enabled us to adjust the pegs on the great wheel of a time machine situated just outside the Master's Common Room in order that the synchronised electric clocks throughout the building agreed upon the moment at which the bells sounded for the change between each study period. Significant events, such as meal times, evening preps, and the hobbies period, were also signalled in this way - a familiar routine to a boy from a nautical school run by bugle calls.

There were occasional problems with ancient wiring running in spaces between floors in the great main building of the school. There were sometimes crises, when my habitual eye on the clocks indicated that the appointed time had been reached, but no bells had sounded. One of us would then race to the master time machine and set off the bells by a switch. This performance, and the ringing of the bells to mobilise the whole school when a fire alarm practice took place at some remarkably inconvenient hour, was accompanied by a sense of power, but this hardly compensated for what was mainly an onerous but useful task.

Joyce Wilson's faith in my ability to progress in the sciences may have been based upon her particular knowledge of my efforts in Chemistry, or her own judgement, for I was by no means entirely devoted to my assignments in these subjects. However, I managed to pass them all in the Higher Certificate at a level sufficient to get the place offered to me at Christ's College, Cambridge, and a scholarship which financed my medical studies for the next five years.

She, in time, became the official Careers Adviser at Bryanston. Her shrewd judgement and astute knowledge of the universities was recognised, although her elaborate make-up and fast cars did not suggest an academic bent, and her taste in fashionable clothes did not include blue stockings. Certainly, I learnt Chemistry easily enough from her, for she had a memorable way of presenting it, but I also learnt how to learn: we read and made notes on a good textbook in our own time, and later we revised from our own notes.

From Cambridge, I wrote to Joyce, addressing her as Miss Wilson, and supplied her with the details of my academic progress. I must have included other pursuits and interests, for she helped to finance a trip to Italy that I took during my first Long Vacation. I bought her a cameo brooch from a little shop on the Ponte Vecchio in Florence. I visited her at home, after her retirement from Bryanston, and my qualification in medicine. We discussed the clinical problems of osteo-arthritis of the hip, which was the nearest we got to a personal topic, but I believe that we both appreciated how much I had gained from her tutorship.

Bill Will

Bryanston inherits some of the grandeur of late Victorian England, for the main building of the school, originally designed by Norman Shaw for the Portman family, is a massive assembly of red brick and Portland stone arranged in a central block, facing south, with two wings which form the sides of a courtyard on the north. The stately front aspect, with the central steps and the terraces leading down to the pond, surrounded by formal lawns, has been likened to a French chateau. The approach to the back is also very striking: the main drive sweeps round the raised mound - known as the 'Plateau' - in a semi-circle, until it suddenly confronts the courtyard. John Betjeman called it 'blood and bandages', and prospecting parents can be in no doubt that they have reached a place of significance. The potential pupil can be overawed - particularly when he is a small boy from Barnardo's who has been selected to take up a bursary place there.

Mindful of the locality of the school the founders had named the various wings and corridors which were to house the first generation of pupils: Dorset, Shaftesbury, and Salisbury, and then included Connaught and Portman, with deference to the indigenous aristocracy. The choice of Hardy for the west wing added an aesthetic element to the topical nomenclature, which I more fully appreciated later on, when I explored in the Cerne Abbas direction, and saw the 'Cross in Hand'.

I was placed in Hardy House under the care of E M Williams, known formally as 'EMW' and by us as 'Bill Will'. He was a graduate from Aberystwyth University, and taught Maths. In his name, his taste for music, and his singsong voice, he reflected well his country of origin. As a bachelor living on the same corridor as our dormitories, he shared our bathrooms and toilets, and, in the morning before breakfast, was to be seen, in his dressing gown, walking from his study-bedroom at one end to his dressing room at the other.

The Bryanston daily programme started with a cold bath and was followed by a brisk run-and-walk around the Plateau. In the summer Bill Will replaced this vigorous commencement to the day with an early morning bathe, which entailed an even brisker walk to and from the River Stour on the southeast boundary of the estate, and I usually joined the group that took this alternative.

It was also compulsory to spend an hour or two outside every afternoon, playing the various seasonal games on three days, and participating in pioneering on the fourth. Bill Williams was in charge of the latter activity, which, for most boys, involved useful maintenance work around the estate, or more enterprising tasks such as building an open-air theatre, or a new boathouse. The fifth afternoon outside was ostensibly a free one, and a good opportunity to walk along the steep riverbank termed the 'Hangings', or climb the surrounding chalk hills above nearby Durweston village.

This rigorous physical side of the Bryanston of the late 1940s was said to be a requisite component of education, as expressed more fully at Gordonstoun School in Scotland, and in Kurt Hahn's School at Salem, Germany, with which Bryanston maintained links. In some manner, the everyday uniform of blue-grey shorts and shirt, and the pioneering, were also part of this aspect of the school, which I took to easily enough after the strict discipline of Barnardo's Russell-Cotes Nautical School.

In sports such as athletics, gymnastics, boxing, and cross-country running, I had previous experience, and easily gained my place in the school teams. In some, I became Captain, and represented Bryanston in the various county and national championships. Bill Williams, I thought, approved of my participation in all of these outdoor activities, particularly when I could contribute to the inter-house competitions, and help to win cups. His identification with Hardy House was strong, but I remember finishing in the inter-house cross-country competition in a position somewhat below that anticipated, both by him and by me, only to hear his disappointment at my attainment exceed by far his appreciation of the good Hardy House team result, under my captaincy.

House prayers replaced the School Assembly once a week, and his contributions to these gatherings were thoughtful, diffident, and occasionally memorable. He spoke once of brothers who had been distinguished members of the school, and, having likened them to thoroughbreds, followed this with the observation that such pupils were often not diligent frequenters of the school as Old Boys - implying that their continued involvement in an active and successful life precluded such nostalgic luxury. It was a shrewd generalisation, which I still respect. In addition to his interest in the successes of Hardy House and his prominent role in the pioneering activities, particularly in the building of the outdoor Greek Theatre, he organised walking and climbing holidays in the Isle of Skye, but I never went on these. In all, I doubt if I moved fully from Barnardo bursary boy to robust Bryanstonian in his view.

Certainly, there were aspects of Bryanston other than physical prowess to which I aspired, and in the earlier part of my time I was rapidly adjusting to ways of living and social habits that were new to me. I admired, and sought to emulate those senior boys in the school who were not only great on the rugby pitch, but were also in the highest classes for their subjects, could play or perform solo with the orchestra, and take a major role in the drama productions for which the school was then becoming well known; these were my schoolboy ideals of 'whole people'.

For the first year or two I remained aware of features such as variations upon the specific blue-grey of the school uniform, the types of casual dress, and the social habits which distinguished bursary boys. Some could also be identified by the address or guardian printed in the School List, of which we all had a copy. However, there was such a remarkable variety of origins and backgrounds among the fee-paying boys that social grouping soon became a matter of shared interests and abilities, rather than origins, as we progressed through the school.

My early physical prowess undoubtedly gave me a sort of reputation among other boys, as well as meeting Bill Williams' interest in the inter-house competitions, but to excel in these particular activities was not quite what I wanted. I saw rugby, rowing, and cricket as the major sports of the school, and I strove hard for my place in these, but never excelled in any of them. I did learn to handle squash and tennis racquets well enough to get around the courts and enjoy the competitiveness of these games, but I knew that I had started to learn them relatively late, and had not the innate skills which I could see in others.

There was a period in my second year during which I formed deep personal friendships, one of which assumed an intensity that made the term time at school the meaningful part of my life, and left holidays as dull and homeless interludes. We were boys of a similar age but of dissimilar backgrounds, and we shared an emotional relationship, which we perceived as a love between friends. We expressed this in the sharing of ideas and affectionate communication, such as I had never experienced before. It permeated my thoughts and began to shape my religious beliefs: "Better love hath no man than this, that a man lay down his life for his friends" I wrote to him. It was undoubtedly a friendship in which affection provoked arousal, and expression would have become more physical had it not been nipped in the bud when the heartfelt letters from me somehow escaped his care and reached the attention of others. Our letters contained very personal expressions to each other, but when mine reached the eyes of people who failed to understand the relationship, I was suddenly afraid. Ultimately, such authorities as housemasters took the matter up, and I felt Bill Williams approached it with more diffidence than understanding. I felt betrayed, and in some way guilty of a friendship which was, in fact, entirely innocent and unexploited. The relationship with the friend was terminated, and that with my housemaster never again assumed any confidence; the incident increased my impression that a parentless bursary boy made him a little uncomfortable.

Many aspects of authority at Bryanston were so very different from those at Russell-Cotes that I had difficulty in identifying with them. The four years in the Nautical School had instilled in me such respect for a discipline based upon physical enforcement that I found the promotion of individual freedom, curtailed only by the minimal restrictions necessary for social tolerance, easy enough to live by, but difficult to adopt. There was no caning, and the commoner forms of punishment such as tidying up the school, or spending a free afternoon running round the quite large school estate, were merely socially inconvenient. The most severe punishment was to be temporarily 'de-membered' from the school, which entailed wearing a white shirt, as opposed to the blue-grey school uniform, losing privileges such as visiting the tuckshop, and throughout each day appearing frequently before the duty school monitor to be checked upon. Offences had to be particularly outrageous to warrant this punishment, and even such crimes as smoking or drinking on the school premises were condemned more for their anti-social aspects than for disobedience to a statutory authority. Within such freedom, authority was more a matter of personal character and confidence, conveyed quietly, than the shouted command, backed by physical force, which had come to me readily enough at the Nautical School.

The first rungs on the ladder of authority in the school were in the favour of each housemaster who, in democratic discussion with those already on it, made the initial appointment of a boy to House Monitor. Contemporaries in Hardy House, with less or similar sports and academic abilities to mine, started up the ladder at a stage quite soon after the time of my emotional friendship affair, but I began the ascent somewhat later. Similarly, I did not acquire an individual study at the School Certificate stage, as did most of my contemporaries with similar academic attainments; I remained in the Hardy Senior Common Room until I was well on the way to the Higher Certificate and University Entry. For a time I wondered if I would be left behind my friends.

My academic work was under the guidance of Joyce Wilson, and although Maths was a subject in which I had enough ability to be in the top sets, it was the relatively gentle Arthur Bull who taught me, not Bill Williams. The latter was not privy to the details of my academic work, therefore, and our relationship developed around my participation in house competitions. I did reach the House Monitor stage in due course, but I never acquired the kind of trusting relationship that I had with my tutor. There was no real antipathy, however, and friendliness persisted beyond my departure from Bryanston.

I last saw him after his retirement from the school to his small home in Blandford. He entertained me to a glass of sherry, and was mildly quizzical of the Barnardo boy who had become a surgeon.

Thor Coade

I was glad to conclude that, if the attention of the Headmaster was ever drawn to the discovered correspondence of my emotional friendship, he thoughtfully overlooked it, for he never mentioned it to me. He was, from the beginning of my time at Bryanston, a figure whom I admired from a distance, and referred to as TFC; Thor Coade I used later, in retrospect, but never Thorold.

At a school in which most staff and boys appeared more concerned with actualities than origins, my own interests and contributions began to reach beyond both academic work and the sports fields. I developed respect and friendship towards boys and members of staff with whom I shared a life that was remarkably broad and deep, and in which the freedom of thought and belief of the individual were paramount.

I walked the nearby hills and talked of ideas and beliefs with other boys. In my last year I shared a study with three others in Hardy House, all on our way to entering the older universities with one form of scholarship or another, but in vastly different subjects - physics, agriculture, music and medicine - so that we learnt to respect each others' different disciplines - and tastes. It was an exciting school in which to be a pupil, and its opportunities were of most importance to those of us who had not similar provisions at home.

We had a fireplace in the study and could burn logs in it that we fetched from the other end of the school. There was little room in the study to store any great quantity and we decided to store them under the floor after cutting a hole in the floorboards for access. The trap door was discovered by the nightwatchman on his rounds, and our doings reported. Our only punishment was the ignominy of carrying the logs to the Masters' Common Room before the trap door was nailed down.

The antidote to specialisation was Humanities. Under this heading, we were taught to look outside our own special subjects and, had I possessed the ability or inclination to become an exclusive scientist, the school would assuredly have prevented me. The timetable of those who spent their last two years in the top Block, preparing for the Higher Certificate, University Entry and Scholarships, had to include other than their main subjects, and for the scientists this meant a weekly Humanities session with the art master, Charles Handley-Reade. He was a lithe figure, with tightly curled ginger hair, a freckled skin, and the reputation of having previously been a student at the school. His exclusive aesthetic image was belied by his considerable ability on the squash courts, and he saw to his mission of educating the school in general, and the senior boy scientists in particular, with infectious commitment. To the former, he introduced the da Vinci Society, and visiting speakers who extolled the virtues of such objects as the great Victorian edifice in which we lived, and the meaning of carved figures in Battersea Park. To the latter, he introduced his message by a public reading of Charles Darwin's lament over his loss of affection for Shakespeare, all in the presence of our concurring biology master, Dick Harthan, before continuing his task at unforgettable sessions in his own room somewhere on an upper corridor. There, he would sit near his gramophone, with its great protruding speaker for conveying His Master's Voice, and with the help of his fine collection of books, introduce us to the colours of the Fauvists, the shapes of the Cubists, and the dreams of the Surrealists at a time when Impressionism had only just reached schoolboy education.

An inclination to piety, and the beginning of some kind of religious experience, had moved me from Victorian moral illustrations to a feeling for earlier devotional art, which was enhanced by gifts of books on the Renaissance in Italy and Holland from one of my benefactors in Barnardo's. Charles Handley-Reade induced me to make time to paint, and I progressed from a murky blue imitation of an anguished scene by George Frederick Watts, through a spontaneous khaki blotch, until some clearer colours emerged; then I knew that I could paint if I tried.

The school was also full of the sound of music, made by its pupils or teachers in various rooms along attic corridors, or by distinguished visiting performers to whom you could listen so closely, in the Centre Room, that you saw the smallest detail of hand movement and heard the rigours of breath control, and came away encouraged. It was in the same Centre Room that the universally enforced half-hour of rest time after lunch could be spent lying across the hard wooden chairs listening to records inserted into an ancient gramophone by some senior boy musicologist, and I still listen to music stretched horizontal.

My own flute playing was undistinguished, and there were others, better than I, ready to play in the school orchestra, but I had some parts in the Inter-House Music Competition groups. Once I was sufficiently touched by the compliments of one adjudicator on the bold opening of a piece by Loillet to overlook his mistaking my second flute part for the first.

The Choral Society provided opportunity for singers less accomplished than those in the School Choir, and when the beginning of co-education brought a weekly visit by girls from Crichel, they not only joined various of our classes, but also contributed sopranos and contraltos to our singing, and attractive partners to our dances and social gatherings. I formed a warm friendship with a dark-haired, gentle girl, who played the violin, and we became affectionate enough to kiss each other goodbye after one of the dances.

In a public school by then renowned for the freedom of expression within its educational system, no one had a more pervasive influence on the development of wholeness than the Headmaster himself did. He presented an exterior of disarming vagueness when he ambled round the school making nonchalant remarks which unwary hearers might misinterpret, but the knowing perceived his depth of understanding of individuals, and their potential for good. I knew his shrewdness of observation from his remarks as he sauntered past the sports notice boards when I was avidly reading them.

His skilful devotion to the production of school plays I enjoyed as a member of an appreciative audience rather than as a performer. I was introduced to not only classic masterpieces and innovative plays fresh from London's West End, but also to the commitment and personal management that made great productions. David Briggs, an ex-choral scholar from Cambridge, who sang base with the School Choral Society, and played trombone in the orchestra, added to his role as second classics master the production of plays in Greek. I took a small part in one of these, more because a friend was playing Bacchus, than for any understanding of the Greek language. This, and a role in a school pantomime produced by Wilf Cowley, gave me some sight and smell of both front and backstage, and the versatility of Bryanston teachers.

The apparent vagueness of Thor Coade that was clearly doffed when it came to producing plays was also discarded when he addressed the school, particularly in full assembly, or on Speech Days. Then he would present a theme in dramatic fashion, and upon one occasion began by shooting an arrow into the centre of a suitably placed target, before discussing worthwhile aims.

It was in the expression of religious belief that I felt that I knew him somewhat more, for there is a small white-painted chapel in the basement of the school which was open at all times for those wishing for quiet and

67

prayer. I knew it well, and particularly on Sunday mornings, when it was used for celebrating Holy Communion. We knelt with the chair in front turned sideways, as a sort of prie-dieu, and the Headmaster, positioned to the front of the small gathering there, did likewise.

I do not know whether it was he, or the school chaplain Jack Winslow, who was primarily responsible for inviting the Franciscans to run an evangelical mission at the school, but I had no doubt that the headmaster believed in Christianity, and was a man of spiritual depth and prayer, as well as an exponent of literary and dramatic art. It became my ambition in some way to emulate these aspects of him rather than be known just as a pupil with athletic prowess, or even as a moderately successful science student. My aspirations in art and music were deeper than I could publicly acknowledge, for my achievements were few.

Towards the end of my fourth year, my tutor must have thought that I might not gain entry to Cambridge. They made arrangements for me to return to school in the autumn, and undertake an exchange with a pupil at Salem, in Germany. In a remarkable manner the links with the headmaster, Kurt Hahn, and the progressive educational system there, had survived the Second World War. The selection of me for this exchange would have been by the Headmaster, in collaboration with my housemaster and tutor, and reflected, I hoped, a little of my academic status and competence in speaking German, as well as my physical prowess.

During the two weeks between the Higher Certificate examinations and the end of term we undertook projects of our own devising that would keep us occupied at no greater expense than being at the school; they were to be fully reported, and judged for a prize. Thus I found myself one evening crossing the Thames on the Woolwich Ferry, while eating fish and chips, and writing my appraisal of the great cathedrals of Salisbury and Winchester, and the new one at Guildford with the semi-relief carving by Eric Gill on its east end. I continued onward, mostly by hitchhiking, to visit Chelmsford, Norwich, Ripon, and York. I omitted Durham, being by then already familiar with that great edifice, and I crossed the north of England overnight in a lorry, which travelled alongside the Manchester Ship Canal in the misty morning. I went to Chester to see the warmth of worn sandstone, before I visited Liverpool to see how our modern cathedral builders could change arches and stonework to a different glory of God. I then had my fill of the 'Three Choirs' cathedrals before returning to Dorset from the west. It was a strenuous expedition to make in only a few days, and when my hand-written report, interlaced with sketches and post-cards, was actually awarded the prize, I hoped that it reflected my level of aesthetic appreciation, as much as my ability to find my way around the country and endure discomfort.

On the way to the final school assembly of that term, I saw the notice promoting me to School Prefect, over the Headmaster's signature. When presented with my prize, accompanied by his shrewd smile, I felt that I had ultimately made something of my time at this big school in the estimation of the person there who most mattered.

EHL

Homeless holidays were the measure of my existence as a schoolboy; my real life was during the term, and at the end of each, I went to various people and places, which provided interludes of recollection. My holidays while in Barnardo's had been very special, for, although my life was that of Euston Hall or Russell-Cotes Nautical School, I still regarded the house of my foster parents as home, and looked forward to being there. At the Nautical School, every endeavour must have been made to get the boys with any kind of home away for the Christmas and summer breaks, despite the wartime difficulties. We travelled by train, wearing our uniform, and carrying other clothes and possessions in a kitbag, like many members of the forces in transit at that time. We knew we were approaching London when we saw the grey glint of the barrage balloons in the sky.

Escorts were provided to take us between the main London terminals, and to see us onto our connecting train. I was met at Princes' Risborough station in Oxfordshire, and there I learnt from my foster father, on a hot sunny day, as we sat in the refreshment room awaiting the little train that went alongside the Chiltern Hills to Watlington, that the most refreshing drink at such a thirst-making time was a really hot cup of tea. Back in the village I joined in the family again, and saw my friends for a week or two, but each time increased the differences between us, and with my uniform clothes and disciplined nautical life, I was less and less a village boy.

Crossing London by underground between Waterloo and Paddington became a familiar routine, and on one return journey I was left at Waterloo station by myself to await the train for Dorset. I found my entertainment at the cinema in the corner where short films and news snippets were shown. At some time during the show I felt a hand on my thigh feeling just below the end of my shorts. I picked up my kitbag and left in some haste, only to notice that my affectionate attender was following me. Not wishing for more attention of this nature I walked out of the station and espied a policeman on Waterloo Bridge. I went up to him and asked the way to somewhere I invented on the spur of the moment, and by the time he had told me the would-be friend had disappeared.

It must have been the intensity of the conflict over London with the arrival of doodlebugs and rockets that caused the cancellation of home leave, in 1945, and I was sent to the camp at Canford, where I received six of the best for stealing apples, which marked my bottom and my memory.

In the 1946 summer I was at Stepney Causeway, being prepared for Bryanston. It was when I was taken to Gorringes, in the West End, to be fitted with the specific dark-blue suit which the school required, that I first realised there was someone in Dr Barnardo's Homes who now had a special responsibility for me - I had acquired a guardian.

When I got to the school I looked at the copy of the School List with which we were all provided. Opposite my name, under the 'parent or guardian' heading, was printed: "E.H.Lucette Esq, c/o 18-26 Stepney Causeway, London, E1". I recognised the address of the Headquarters of Barnardo's, and the name as the important General Superintendent to whose office I had delivered mail when I was the office boy, but there was no mention of Dr Barnardo's Homes in the address. This was the first of many acts of thoughtfulness by which he showed that he knew what was important to a boy at a public school.

Each holiday, while at Bryanston, I would break my return trip to school, through London, and take the underground to Aldgate East, and then a trolley bus along the Commercial Road to the Troxy Cinema, just opposite to the street with the Headquarters, which I had known so well. I was concerned always to be in good time, and, having mastered the vicissitudes of the public transport, usually had a few minutes to spare when I presented myself to the porter at the main entrance. He always greeted me with great courtesy, and invited me to sit on one of the benches in the main entrance, so that I could gaze at the 'Ever Open Door' while he let my guardian know that I had arrived. When called up to his office, I knew my own way through the tortuous corridors and stairways, and would find him behind his desk.

He was grey and eminent; his suit, with a long lapel crossing a broad expanse of chest and abdomen, was grey, and the closely- curled hair above his thoughtful brow was grey; but his eyes were of a deeper colour, and, although well hooded, so that I could not easily tell his thoughts or mood, they would appear with either deep humour or interrogation when the lids lifted. As for his eminence, it was soon clear that, as the General Superintendent, he had the immediate responsibility for the whole management of the Homes, and I gathered, more gradually, that he had previously been a distinguished member of the Colonial Service, as a judge in Ceylon, as Sri Lanka was then called. My school reports were always before him, and since there was usually insufficient amiss to provide a topic for our regular confrontation, he would discuss cricket, books, and, later on, ethics. Although always direct with his compliments, he gave only indirect advice.

For many of the half-term holidays at Bryanston, I was one of that small group of boys without readily available parents or relatives, who would stay in the school, with the solace of wearing my corduroy trousers and maroon sweater, and wandering freely through that great building, or the grounds. Sometimes, however, I had a very particular visitor from the Homes, in the shape of Miss Mary Carlyle: a lady of uncertain age, with the privileged background of Oxford and Kensington, and a family name which even I associated with the academic world of literature and history. Her position as the Head of the Education Department of the Homes may have provided the ostensible reason for her visits, but this was never apparent from the way in which she bowled into the courtyard of the school in an open-top sports car, accompanied by her sister. They behaved as two middle-aged spinster aunts visiting one of their favourite nephews. Their interest in the school was enthusiastic and fervent, and they never left without taking me out to one of the surrounding villages where we could have a strawberry and cream tea, sitting in a sunny garden. The relationship must have gone well beyond any concepts of duty, for I not only visited them at their Victorian apartment in Kensington, but also periodically received gifts of books from their own library, which were valuable works on art or literature, and often had some front-plate reflecting their distinguished family back-ground.

From the beginning of my time at Bryanston, it was clear that my guardian was to provide somewhere for me to stay in the holidays, and that it was not expected of my foster-mother to provide for a boy at a public school. Quite early in my time there it was arranged that I should spend a holiday with a couple in a bungalow in Surrey. He was the Reverend K P Stewart, a clergyman who visited academic establishments around the country to tell them about the work done by the Homes - in the form of a Sunday sermon, to judge by his visits to Bryanston. He was, as such, an important fund-raiser. He had no children of his own, but doubtless was supposed to be familiar with the wants and ways of schoolboys; I found him unbending and unattractive. His wife, whom I knew to be the sister of Derek Wigram, a master at Bryanston who later became headmaster of Monkton Coombe, appeared gentle and subservient.

They were kind to me, but I felt constrained, and on formal behaviour, and I obtained most enjoyment by going on long cycle-rides by myself, around the country. On one of these I made my way over many miles to visit Peg Dovey, the ex-Matron from Russell-Cotes Nautical School who had remained a friend to me. I was caught by nightfall, and slept, somewhat fitfully, in a road-mender's shelter beside a railway line. I recall no reprimand over this prolonged cycle trip, but I was deeply hurt when the clergyman upbraided me for preceding his wife into a railway carriage when we were boarding a train; I was upset to have my lack of manners so emphasised at a time when I was learning how to behave in a culture to which I had not been born or brought up.

At this stage I must have been regarded as some kind of 'Winslow boy' by those responsible for my position at the school, for, on one afternoon during a holiday, I was taken to meet a distinguished man called Mr MacAndrew. He was busily chopping down silver birch trees on his estate, and he invited me to help him. In his position as a Governor of Bryanston, he was in some way involved with the arrangement whereby Dr Barnardo's Homes had a bursary place there. I was aware that the current occupant of this place was being shrewdly inspected, as the trees were being felled, and that I was not found too greatly wanting.

The holiday placements made for me between my first few terms had much to do with the Homes and some of the distinguished people who worked for them at that time. Dr Gilmore, their Medical Officer, who had also come from the Colonial Service, invited me to join him and his son for a sailing trip on the Norfolk Broads. I was more at home with the sailing boat than I was with their kind of life, but it proved a happy holiday during which I had an easy friendship with both father and son, despite the latter's position, somewhat senior to mine, at Haileybury, a considerably more conventional public school.

It was a photograph from that holiday which remained on the board in my guardian's office for some years. It showed me, quaintly dressed, and looking thoughtful; it continued to remind me of how I had entered a life so very different from the life at sea which had pre-occupied my thoughts and ambitions until the age of fourteen.

In time my guardian found some parents in contact with the Homes who wanted a companion for their only son, Peter. The Johansens lived in an old cottage perched on a small hill next to the woods of a country estate near Newbury, in Berkshire. Indeed, it was said to have been the home of the estate manager, and was a lovely house with brick tiling on its front, overlooking a lawn that sloped down to a disused tennis court, beyond a magnificent cedar tree. The back of the house looked across a sunken lane to a great beech wood. They were some half a mile from their nearest neighbour, and even further from utility supplies: water was pumped up from the well in the kitchen, and lighting was by paraffin lamps, or from a carbide acetylene plant in a shed down the garden. There were chickens and ducks to look after, eggs to collect, an orchard of old fruit trees, and a paddock down the hill with no animals grazing in it - but it had an old pump house which had been used to fill tanks in the attic of the cottage with fresh water. The Johansens possessed a great black Labrador dog that loved to walk the surrounding countryside as much as I did.

Mr Johansen was an engineer with the local government, and it was agreed that I should call him by his first name, Tony, but I hardly ever did so. When his work during holiday time entailed visits to the laboratories of the Ministry of Agriculture, development sites, or other interesting places, he would take me with him. His training had made him precise, and he taught me lettering, woodwork, metalwork, and left the indelible impression of how a man's workshop should be organised. His wife, Rachel, was a physiotherapist who continued a little local practice. Having spent her earlier years at The Mount – a Quaker boarding school in York - and trained thereafter in London hospitals, she easily supported a youngster moving towards the study of medicine who needed a termly appraisal of his clothes, books, and games requirements. She also had played the violin, and provided me with music which I could play on my flute, and, as a writer of children's stories, she knew a deal about books, so that I could easily talk to her of my thoughts and interests. I called her Bunty, which was a nickname from the time when she had her maiden name of Hunt.

The Johansens were the first family of professional status I had ever known at all intimately, and their acquired parental role and interest in my school life became so important that I became very fond of them, and began to look forward to holidays with more enthusiasm. Their son was of my own size, but a year or two younger, and I provided unfair competition rather than good companionship for him.

I had my own little room in the cottage, which looked out upon the great wood across the lane. Amid the quietness there, or often while walking miles through the countryside, I could reflect on the events of an increasingly busy term time. Bunty knew about boarding schools; she understood my life and would share in it, but never could I discuss my earlier childhood, or my time spent in Dr Barnardo's Homes with her. On the other hand, it was the only place where I could, occasionally, drop the formalities of good behaviour, and express a feeling of disgruntlement, or an even darker humour, without losing their affection. I came to feel that they loved me almost as parents, and for a while I considered their house to be my home, but I never addressed them by parental names.

Only once did they visit me at school, and then the pride of showing them round, as other boys did with their parents, was tempered by the sense that they might see it as a better schooling than they had for their own son, and that their attention to me could oust him. Certainly, something changed in my relationship with the Johansens, and for the Christmas of 1949, and the Easter of 1950, my homeless holidays were spent elsewhere.

The most important visitor I had at school was my guardian himself. He had consented to come for the Speech Day during my second year, when I was featuring prominently in the gymnastics display and other events arranged to enhance such occasions. Anticipation of this great opportunity to show him my achievements in the school must have been behind my disappearance to the sanatorium a few days before, with a strange illness marked by a fever. During one night I lay sleepless from dusk to dawn, occupied by thoughts of impending catastrophe. I recovered in time to be on my feet to meet him, but, having missed the final rehearsals, it was as a spectator that I took him round, and explained what my participation was to have been. He never in any way expressed disappointment, or dwelt on my feeling of failure, and this was the beginning of my deep respect and distant affection for him as a detached and philosophical person, responsible for a boy who always endeavoured, and sometimes achieved.

At the end of my fourth year, having left Bryanston with the expectation of returning the following term for the exchange with the School at Salem, in Germany, I arranged to get myself and my few possessions to the camp at Wooler in Northumberland, there being no longer a home for me in Berkshire. Camping with the Franciscans in Northumberland during the previous summer holiday had been so happy an experience that I was glad to return there, and to remain afterwards in that part of England. For a few weeks I joined the staff that ran residential courses for the National Association of Boys Clubs at Ford Castle. It was to there that the news of a place at Christ's College, Cambridge, came and I suddenly grew from schoolboy to student. Commensurate with the prospect of a new life I took to writing poetry, earnest discussions, playing bridge, smoking cigarettes, and drinking ale.

<u>Composed upon the bank of the Tweed just below The</u>
<u>Border Bridge at Berwick.</u>

Mud banks appear in the seaward–flowing river,
Water sinks lower on the stonework bridge.
Tide is ebbing.

Lamplighter walks the riverside beacons,
Curfew clangs slowly for the setting sun,
Day is ending.

Industry encroaches on the one-time seaport.
Curfew and gas lamps will go like the rest.
Times are changing.

Nations succumb to the dialectic monster,
Material status usurps true love,
Community progress is mother to reason,
Naught's an offspring of something above.
Faith's retreating.

Arrangements were made for me to return
southwards and present myself and my academic status to
the Director of Education for Berkshire, since this was the
only county to which I had some kind of claim as a
resident. After a discussion of El Greco's painting of 'The
Burial of Count Orgaz' in the National Gallery, and of
Aldous Huxley's views on the painter, I was awarded a full
County Major Scholarship. This provided the funds
whereby I studied medicine for the next five years, but
during the holidays, which now became vacations, I had to
supplement my income with a variety of employments.

Mr Lucette undertook my preparation for
Cambridge by seeing me through a visit to his own East
End tailor, who measured me for a formal evening suit,
after asking me on which side I dressed – a question
which I needed a little help to answer. He then increased
the significance of one of our meetings in his office by
handing me my Barnardo folder to read. I saw firstly that

my birth certificate stated my mother's name, Ann Brocklehurst, and my father's as 'Fred Davis (putative)'. I thought of the Latin verb *putare*, and wondered if the entry merely reflected doubts in the mind of some crusty Registrar in a Liverpool office, or my mother had attempted to protect someone; she was aged seventeen at that time, and had been 'in service' at a family home. She had given birth to me in what was clearly a Catholic Nursing Home, and the nuns had arranged my care by another family, since she could not look after me. I understood that I was much loved by this first foster mother, but matters of faith and finance led to my admission to the Liverpool 'Ever Open Door' of Dr Barnardo's Homes. There then followed the records of my mother's inability to pay much towards my support, and my placement in my Oxfordshire foster home. I could deduce the reason for birthday presents having reached me there from two people signing themselves as my mother for a year or two, but doubtless time and the anonymity arrangements had curtailed these contacts. I made notes of a few details, and handed the folder back.

I was then invited to stay with my guardian at his home, and I felt that this was a privilege related to my having finished successfully at Bryanston and gained a place at Cambridge University. I met his wife for the first time, and during a dinnertime discussion concerning the role of England within its dwindling Empire, made it clear that I favoured our withdrawal from the colonies. This provoked her imperial ardour and a rebuke to a young man with no ambition to retain our hard-won possessions; it was a salutatory reminder of how much of their lives had been given to the Colonial Service, and of how little my guardian had told me of this. It was at his home that I first saw him as a family man, and I admired his stately figure as he sat one evening at his piano, gently playing Chopin.

Nor did his guardianship stop with my entry into a relatively independent university student life, for he still saw me periodically, and he enabled me to purchase an ebonite concert flute, which had become available from a fellow student. We still discussed my prospects, and when I talked to him of my involvement with Anglo-Catholicism and the Franciscans to the point of wishing to join them as a member of the Third Order, he merely mentioned Andre Gide's 'Strait is the Gate'. I read the book and deepened my perception of the straitened life of love and service. Not only did I refrain from undertaking the particular solemn vows required of members of the Franciscan Third Order, despite my attraction to the concept of living the religious life from within the world, but I also became aware that such constraints might prove inadequate as I continued to study medicine.

Following my start at Cambridge, he arranged that I spent my vacations with Peggy Steadman at her home in the Little Boltons, a terrace of cream-coloured houses in London SW, with steps up to the front door covered by a square 19th century porch of some grandeur, and a capacious basement. She was a prominent worker in the Barnardo Helpers League, with a wide knowledge of both Cambridge and London. The flat at the top of the house, and the room next to mine, were rented to young people with interesting London jobs, and I was able to do my own holiday jobs from there. I also got to know the Earls Court, Chelsea and Kensington areas well by walking them between underground stations and buses, and I acquired the social life of a student in London. In the early mornings I could find a church within walking distance where I could attend and sometimes assist at the Mass. St Paul's, Knightsbridge, had that kind of dated Anglo Catholicism which I liked, and attracted to its small congregation a soberly-dressed poet and author whom I knew to have been once a bank-clerk; I already admired his poems and plays, and knew his professed Anglo Catholic churchmanship. At times I wandered around the many quiet roads, squares and gardens in that part of London, and I could easily reach the river around the Chelsea Embankment, or the museums, great shops, and concert halls of the West End. I thought of the artists and writers who had lived around there in the past, and the many interesting people I met there at that time, and I greatly liked it.

I saw little of my landlady, and even less of her husband, who occasionally appeared when on holiday from school teaching. In time he became an even rarer visitor, and the house appeared to be run by the landlady and her friend. In discussing these holiday arrangements with my thoughtful guardian, who doubtless had some hand in them, I ventured observations influenced by Freudian views, which I had by then acquired. He referred me to Carl Jung, but I was slow to see the social implications of my position there. Certainly, much was made of my success as a student at Cambridge, and my showing as a budding doctor, but I did not see these as social achievements. Perhaps, as the ward of her superior in the Barnardo organisation, I had more of her sympathy than she did of mine, for by then I no longer sought a home for my holidays, and was grateful to have such comfortable lodgings, and a good landlady.

That arrangement lasted but briefly, and it was followed by a period during which I became more intimately involved with Dr Barnardo's Homes again. A room was found for me in Mossford Lodge - the house at Barkingside, in Essex, in which the Founder of the Homes had lived, and around which he had developed a Village Home for Girls. I already knew a little of the place, for Dr Gilmore, who took me for the sailing holiday on the Norfolk Broads, had lived there. I had also spent a few days in the little hospital, having my adenoids removed, for it had been decided that some chest pain and cough which I had at school would be helped by such a manoeuvre, and it was organised through the Homes. Like the Boys Garden City, through which I had passed some few years earlier, the Girls Village Home had been evacuated and greatly altered in function during the Second World War. When I began to spend my holidays there, part of it was used as a transit place, particularly for groups of children on their way to Australia as emigrants.

I was given the vacation task of helping with the supervision of one of these parties of children, and spent a few days endeavouring not to lose any of them while we conducted them around London as they made their preparations somewhat excitedly.

I had already some experience in helping younger children in various social activities, both with the Franciscans, and at a boys club in the Battersea district of London run by Christ's College, where it seemed easy enough to help the boys there with boxing and other sports. My slightly self-conscious efforts there paled beside those of a friend from Christ's who, having failed to meet the requirements of the regular Army, was destined to join the Church to become an Army chaplain, and showed his military interests by a display of his collection of old swords; to the boys he was a swashbuckling hero. I helped in the running of a camp for the same boys on the south coast, and found myself with youngsters who had never seen hens as the producer of eggs, and thought it right to pocket those which were lying around on the farm. It was easier for me to identify with these boys than to provide them with authoritative guidance.

The most mortifying experience of working with younger children was when I accepted the offer of a holiday job at one of the Dr Barnardo's Homes that was short of staff. It was run by a middle-aged couple along lines, which I knew from my own experience to be traditional, in that the staff lived and fed separately from the boys, and maintained their aloof authoritarian position. I was expected to be part of this arrangement, as a member of the staff, but I felt myself to be more in sympathy with the young inmates. One morning, I came into the dormitory and could smell tobacco smoke, and while interrogating them to discover the smokers, became annoyed by their denials, and reported them to the superintendent. He then requested me to discharge the recognised punishment of six strokes of the cane across the bottoms of the two offenders. I did as ordered, but found the experience so upsetting that I was glad to leave the Home a day or two later, and, as I stood on the platform awaiting my train, I felt guilty of having betrayed the boys.

It became clear that whatever inclination I had to redeem my own childhood by caring for homeless children, it was not to be met within the organisation of the Homes. Nor could I follow a Christian calling with the evangelical zeal shown by their Founder, but as I lived at that time in the room that had been his study, I quite often thought of him. Clearly he had committed himself; he had actually done things for children despite the circumstances of his time, and I was among those who had benefited from this. I was visited at Mossford Lodge one day by an elderly clergyman, the Reverend Snowden-Smith, who had known my room as Barnardo's study from the time when they had worked there together. He reflected a little on the Doctor's personality and views. Thereafter, I developed a personal respect for him, which was beyond my more critical appreciation of his evangelical, charitable and sociological activities. Looking at the ornate woodwork around the mantelpiece over the fireplace one day, as doubtless he had done many a time, I suddenly recognised his compassion, and with this came a strong feeling of gratitude. I thought that I might be the first child enabled by his service to become a doctor, and by being a good doctor, respond to his caring.

It was doubtless the increasing commitment to medical studies rather than any distinguished academic achievements that gained my guardian's continued approval, for he in no way discouraged my relatively premature proposal to get married, and accepted an invitation to the wedding. At the point when the bridegroom expresses appreciation of his family support, I spoke of his thoughtful guardianship during my life at Bryanston, and as a medical student. He acknowledged my gratitude with disarming diffidence.

Soon thereafter he retired from his Barnardo post, and my supervision was taken over by Theodore Tucker, his successor. By that time I was well on the way to qualifying, and found the necessity of accounting to him for my financial support quite irksome. I wrote:

'A young man of goodly intent
Kept accounts of all that he spent.
At a large overdraft,
He just simply laughed,
"I know precisely where it all went"'

To which he replied:
'Pounds, shillings and pence,
Where, whither and whence?
You write it all down
Then each half a crown,
Is spent with good common sense'

Having married while still a medical student, qualification, followed by appointment to a houseman's post at Guy's, with a regular, albeit meagre, income, was a welcome achievement, and my ties with Barnardo's became a matter of contacts through the After Care Department, which I maintained with some diligence. My appreciation of their support was matched by their reflections on my progress.

I was well on my way to specialisation as a surgeon when I last visited Mr Lucette and his wife. He had, by then, suffered illness, and much sadness within his family life, but he remained thoughtfully attentive. Having expressed his pride in my progress and admiration of the path that I had chosen, he bade me farewell with his customary courtesy, and I never saw him again.

Brother Michael

Finding a Father was difficult. The personal one to whom I had turned at lonely times in the Homes was the same one that I trusted, as advised by the Bulldog preacher ("Trust in the Lord with all thy heart, and lean not under thine own understanding; in all thy ways acknowledge Him, and He will direct thy path") and He could be resorted to in times of doubt. This kind of personal belief in a Father did not enable me to express in any public manner a belief in the God presented to me thus far - a severe and distant individual concerned with sin and salvation, slightly more approachable when praying in a church.

The Chaplain during my first few terms at Bryanston was Jack Winslow, a stocky man who appeared permanently sun-tanned, and the smooth skin of his bald head contrasted strikingly with his wrinkled face. Among his less spiritual tasks was our instruction in sex and, offsetting this association with an embarrassing topic, he had great personal charm, acquired no doubt from his schooling at Eton and Oxford. He had also served in India within a Brotherhood that identified with the native way of life, and from thence he brought a sense of Eastern mysticism. His ideals were absolute beauty, goodness and truth, as espoused in the Moral Re-Armament movement, and at the humanitarian level he sympathised with the Mahatma Ghandi, and with the Society of St Francis, the Anglican Franciscan movement which had started by working among the unemployed, homeless, and wayfarers in this country, following the Great Depression.

I associated Jack Winslow with the particular impact of the whitewashed chapel in the basement at Bryanston. It had no windows, and the simple cross on the stone altar was strikingly projected against the pure white alcove behind, when the lights were first turned on, for it was always open, and a place to which I resorted to

85

think and pray. It was there that Jack Winslow donned his chasuble to celebrate the Holy Communion against the whiteness, early on Sunday mornings, and I became one of a small band that shared the peace and quietness of that basement chapel. My Father at that time was a God of solace and comfort.

The strong charm of Jack Winslow so engulfed some senior boys in the school - those whom I respected for their great prowess on the sports field and their academic and artistic achievements - that they made personal confessions of belief in the God that he portrayed. These were memorable, particularly when they took place in the middle of a service broadcast on the radio, but such confessions were not asked of juniors at my level. Indeed, I had no intimate discussions with him, although I felt somehow identified with the visiting preacher who came every term or two, and preached to the whole school on behalf of Dr Barnardo's Homes.

It was doubtless Jack Winslow's association with the Anglican Franciscans that resulted in a mission to the school during which I first began to know a Father, through the eyes of a Brother named Michael. He wore a brown habit girdled with a white rope in which three knots were tied, and, standing on the raised dais addressing the crowd of boys in the Centre Room, he was attractive. Ostensibly, he was the assistant on the mission run by his Father Superior, Algy Robertson SSF (Society of St Francis) - a small rotund friar with his own way of persuading us that his Father was important.

Michael, as the younger member of the mission team, invited personal contact. I went to see him and soon came to know him as a lovable friend with whom I could talk of books, pictures, music, people, thoughts, feelings, sex, myself, and occasionally of God. His own love of God was seen easily in his love of people, among whom I became a favoured and privileged one.

Following the mission to the school, a group of us cycled across the countryside to visit their Friary a few miles away, near Cerne Abbas, where we joined with them in their prayers and offices. It was a quiet and beautiful place, consisting of a collection of farm-like buildings around a courtyard, off which were the chapel and refectory, all set just below the hills across which Tess of the D'urbervilles would have walked. Up there, we found orchids growing on the chalky soil, and could see in the distance a grotesque giant carved on the hillside. Around the Friary, we met the friars who filled such offices as Brother Secretary and Brother Steward, and a few other residents remaining from the early mendicant days of the Anglican Franciscans. We sat with them at the silent mealtimes in the refectory, and listened to a sonorous reading from some devotional book, or, occasionally, a strikingly witty literary piece.

I came to know quite a few of these remarkable men, and even retreated to the Friary for times of quiet recollection and prayer. I learnt through them about a God who was essentially a loving Father approached through adoration, contrition, thanksgiving, and the offer of service. The first way increasingly led me into the liturgy of the catholic Church, as practised in the Church of England, and I became deeply involved in the process of redemption acted out in the Mass. The second way taught me self-analysis and confession, and the experience of forgiveness that safeguards against the desolation of being proven so very inadequate. Thirdly, through the warm, affectionate, but never indulgent relationship with Brother Michael, I came to know other active and attractive Christians, some of whom were in or about to join the priesthood or religious orders, and I was thankful. Fourthly, it was also recognised that, among these relatively religious Christians, I had the calling, or vocation, to become a doctor, rather than primarily a priest, or member of a religious order, and that this was to be my service.

I went with the Friars to a camp in Northumberland, after which we made a pilgrimage over the countryside where St.Cuthbert of Lindisfarne had travelled, pulling with us a cart with our few necessities for sleeping and feeding. At the various stopping places we performed a play by Laurence Houseman or Andre Gheon, concerned with the life of the church and its renewal by building. The pilgrimage ended with our performance of the play in the Galilee chapel at the western end of Durham cathedral, followed by a solemn procession to St. Cuthbert's tomb. The dusty and tired pilgrims were the guests of ecclesiastics around the Cathedral Close. Canon A M Ramsay and his gentle wife entertained us to tea, during which I came to admire this remarkable man, distinguished by his erudition, and a friendly twinkle in his eye.

The Church in the North of England became familiar to me, with its Celtic origins around the Borderlands and the Isle of Lindisfarne, and the Farnes – all part of the route of early evangelism, stretching from Iona to the Emerald Isle. There it was possible to feel a history prior to the Romanisation of our Church, and this encouraged in me independence from Rome and from the common impression that being catholic in Churchmanship meant, ultimately, a desire to become a Roman Catholic.

The summer holiday, 1950, during which I changed from schoolboy to university student, had begun with my second visit to the Franciscan camp beside the Cheviot Hills in Northumberland, followed by the pilgrimage. The news of a good Higher Certificate and a place at Cambridge came through while I was still in Northumberland, working for the National Association of Boys Clubs, at Ford Castle. A rapid metamorphosis, aided by my guardian, and a County Major Scholarship, saw me established in a room at the top of the V staircase in the Third Court of Christ's college by the beginning of Autumn Term.

I shared with a student somewhat older than I, and, remarkably, he was reading theology in preparation for the priesthood. Who again had ensured an arrangement that so clearly favoured my welfare? It was not that Rex Howe was actually one of the band of Franciscan-orientated Christians among whom I had already found friends, but he was a mature student, who had served in the armed forces and seen a deal of the working world before coming up to Cambridge to read theology. He was committed firmly to 'high' Anglo-Catholicism, and while I was considering the nature of Authority in the Church, he was more perplexed with the rudiments of Hebrew and Greek, which he now had to face.

Brother Michael was also by then at Cambridge, in Westcott House, as an ordinand preparing to become a priest, and through him I met many more Christians with whom I shared interests in art, music, buildings, and even sport, as well as a thoughtful approach to Christianity, the Church, and above all, to other people.

I went on missions with the Friars, and while with the hop-pickers in Kent, where we picked enough hops to earn our own subsistence, I played my flute for the outdoor services, and I was taken to a nearby abbey of an enclosed Order of nuns, in order to meet the Lady Abbess and talk with her through a grill. She seemed both holy and remarkably shrewd, to a young and homeless student. I also made a retreat in the sombre house of the Cowley Fathers, in Westminster, met a Benedictine monk from Nashdom, and spent a Holy Week with the Community of the Resurrection, at Mirfield. There we followed the dark sequence of the Passion in prayers and sombre devotions, stage by stage, until the crucifixion was over, and then we fled the great chapel, leaving it empty of music and bared of adornments. Over Saturday it was cleaned, prepared, and decorated for the great festival of the Resurrection, which was proclaimed there with liturgical splendour on Easter morning.

Finding a Father in a God worshipped through a beautiful liturgy and music, in great and lovely buildings, made adoration easy, and through fellow Christians fatherhood and brotherhood were learnt within companionships which were warm and sensitive, so that adulation followed. Increasingly, I was attracted to both the religious life and the priesthood.

My brotherly friar was not yet a priest, and although the only one among a crowd of Christian friends with whom I could talk frankly, personally, and in confidence, he was not my Father Confessor, nor did I ever really find one, but I did undertake confession regularly.

It was my habit as a student to share interests with many, and confidences with few. Within Dr Barnardo's Homes our common lot had been to find parenting from those in charge of us, and friendship from each other; our affections survived somewhere between these two. We developed our own language and ethos, but our personal history formed no part of this. My entry to Bryanston was an opportunity to change my plight, but not my history; that was a matter for disregard by me and everyone else. The education there was in objectives, not origins. The awareness of being a bursary boy from Barnardo's was not made apparent to me or by me. In most of my friendships it never obtruded, and I accounted for my parentless childhood and homelessness by being guarded, or even evasive, but I did not overtly fabricate explanations; real friends knew how not to enquire too far. My awareness was more of the need to avoid eliciting sympathy, or even notoriety, than of bearing shame for my past.

Affections, which had grown only slowly before I left Russell Cotes, became more powerful at Bryanston, motivating personal friendships, and activating my intellectual interests. While the former approached overt homosexuality, and the latter religious devotion of some depth, it was the relationship with Michael Fisher that introduced a balance between the *eros* and *agape* of love. In this relationship, I confided over my childhood at an early stage.

Thanksgiving came easily enough among such companions, for it stemmed from the awareness of being loved personally, individually, and absolutely.

The way of service for me in the Church, however, meant that I had to consider my own vocation - or calling, and for a time the priest seemed more attractive than the doctor. A first step was to join the Third Order of the Franciscans, and it was in discussing this with my guardian that he acquainted me with Andre Gide's 'Strait is the Gate'. Having read it, I accepted that the way of loving God was more likely to be a difficult matter, than one easily defined, and was inseparable from loving mankind.

Furthermore, I had a certain reluctance to accept too defined an ecclesiastical authority. This arose during my later time at school, when my reading had moved from Huxley to the Russian writers. I had noted how one of the Karamazov brothers relates the story of the Grand Inquisitor's visit to the jail where the custodians had realised they had a re-appeared Christ incarcerated. During the confrontation the Inquisitor explains Christ's mistake when he refused the Devil's temptation to turn stones to bread - He could have fed the perpetual hunger for belief and conviction. It was the function of the Catholic Church to answer this hunger with infallible doctrine which all would believe in, and Christ had to go. At the time, I saw it as the presentation of Russian Orthodoxy versus Roman Catholicism, and it counteracted a very strong temptation to accept an authority infallible in doctrine and morals. Indeed, when I read the writings of a number of the great mystics of the church, I felt more sympathy with their doubts than their devotion, and 'dark nights of the soul' I understood.

At university, I joined those debates at the Union on topics important to Christians, such as apartheid, the Central African Federation of States, and the occasional formal Catholic disputation. I also became a member of the Student Christian Movement, identifying more easily with its wide approach to belief and practice, rather than with more specific organisations which required a stated personal belief following conversion, such as the Roman Catholics on the one hand, or the Intercollegiate Christian Union on the other. However, I had no compunction in coming forward to state my beliefs at a mission service in London, run by the great American Evangelist, Dr Billy Graham.

Presented with so many ways of being a Christian, I preferred to worship and pray within the liturgical tradition of the Anglican Franciscans, as practised in their ancient Saxon church, St. Benet's, in Cambridge, rather than with the more elaborate high church liturgy which my room companion, Rex, found at 'Little' St Mary's.

Within the college, attendance at the dark-panelled chapel seemed formal, and included reading lessons from a great brass lectern, and listening to academic sermons, but I had a warm friendship with the Irish chaplain, John Brown, and, through him, came to know Dr Peck, a Fellow of the College and a classicist who delivered the University Orations in Latin. He was also a fervent High Churchman who could just be seen amid the clouds of incense around the altar of Little St.Mary's on Sunday mornings when he served as Subdeacon for the High Mass. Furthermore, he was a prominent figure in the Morris Dance movement associated with the socialist interest in the revival of rural crafts around Thaxted and

East Anglia, and an authority on lampposts in Cambridge; it was a privilege to know such a truly eccentric don.

Joyce Wilson, my tutor from Bryanston, not only continued her interest in me, but also provided me with funds for a trip to Italy, organised by a group of Christians, including Brother Michael. The intention was to make our devotions to St. Francis at Assisi, but we also included Florence and Rome in our itinerary, and saw the great churches, sculptures, and pictures which I had already heard of, and many others.

Our time in Assisi was particularly reverent as we saw The Carcere where St Francis had lived, and the little church of San Damiano, which he had restored, now enclosed in the great basilica. We saw his life shown in the simple frescoes, glorious in colour, and great in power, and we prayed to the little saint. We also enjoyed the cheerful hospitality of some nuns there, who showed us how to cook snails using an old-fashioned flat iron.

There must have been some ecumenical ecclesiastical organisation behind our pilgrimage, for when we got to Rome, we were invited to an audience with the Pope. Clad in motley holiday garb, we looked unprepared and out of place as we gathered with many others in the first great antechamber of the Vatican Palace. We were somewhat surprised to be selected out and taken to the next chamber, and then further selected, and passed through a number of chambers, until we were in the one next to that occupied by His Holiness as he gave special audience to a few high dignitaries and beautifully-clad members of distinguished Catholic families, who went into him. He then came out into our chamber and, after the previous prolonged display of colourful pomp and ceremony, his white-clad simplicity was very impressive as he walked around and talked to us. He enquired from whence we came, and, when he heard Oxford among the many answers, replied: "Ah! I have the Oxford Dictionary".

In Florence, we were amidst such a plethora of things we wanted to see that we systematically kept a siesta each early afternoon, during which one of our members read from a classical Victorian guide book, before we went forth to renew our visits. I was impressed by the great architectural work of Brunelleschi and also particularly moved by the simple beauty of a glazed semi-relief profile of the young St John on the cloister wall of a monastery across the river. It was on the Ponte Vecchio, where Rossetti had Dante meet Beatrice, that I found a small stall from which I was able to buy a simple cameo brooch for my school time tutor, Joyce Wilson.

I brought back, with great care, a large photograph of Donatello's David, from the Uffizi Collection, for myself. It was framed to hang in my sitting room when I returned to college to begin my second year by moving into lodgings in town, just beyond Christ's Pieces. My landladies were the unmarried eldest and youngest of a local family of sisters, and exercised their sense of propriety as they diligently cared for their young student, for, when I returned after the Christmas vacation, they had moved the picture to a position covered by the open door, and therefore not visible to a casual inspection of the room. The lithe figure, beautiful and nude, must have worried their sensibilities as it stood with one foot firmly on Goliath's head.

The move to lodgings left me without my cheerful and robust room companion of the previous year, and I was keeping only my own company for the first time since the period in London before entering Bryanston. I felt the loneliness, and my thoughts were often with a younger boy with whom I had become recently friendly. It was initially a relationship of patronage, for I was introduced to him when he had just started at Bryanston, as someone who could perhaps help him in a brotherly fashion, for he also was from Dr Barnardo's Homes. I soon became aware of the strong sexual feelings that the relationship aroused, and I felt that any expression of these would betray the trust within it. I had also by then enough awareness of my attraction to one or two girls whom I had come to know to see some kind of dilemma arising.

It was with a little advice and a lot of temerity that I went to talk to a remarkable man, who was not only a theologian, authority on church history, college don, and high-church priest, but also an American, with considerable experience in psychological counselling. For all this, he talked little and listened carefully, with the expertise that enabled me to give some account of my feelings, of my childhood and time in the Homes, of my relationships and reactions as a boy in a boarding school, and of my more recent relationships, particularly within the church, and among fellow Christians. There were a few sessions, all of similar pattern, and they took place in his comfortable rooms in Caius College, of which he was the Dean. He, rather than I, sat on the sofa, and while he listened, and made occasional leading comments, I came to see my feelings and affections for what they were, and the complex urges became less; there was a kind of dying of a whole part of me, and with this I lost a lot of my affection for Christian friends, particularly my brotherly Friar, and even for my fatherly God. It was a form of self-analysis, not deep analysis, nor did it need associations to bring out the significance of my particular birth, childhood, and up-bringing, but it was a series of quite short lessons from which I gained a valuable ability to see myself, whenever I remembered to stop and do so. Each session would end when the bell sounded for Hall, and he would stand up, put out his cigarette, and put on his gown, before going down to dine; I would go out to the street, and back to my own college.

Soon after this psychotherapeutic episode my changed relationships included the girlfriend who, a year or two later, joined me in marriage, and I became more single-minded in my study of medicine. I grew away from

Michael, and my Franciscan friends. He became, in due course, a widely known missionary, a leader of the Anglican Franciscans, and ultimately a Bishop. I saw him again, in later life, after our ways had widely diverged, and he was respectful, but a little surprised, I thought, at the course I had taken. I found him by then to be a wise church elder, but to me he remained Brother Michael.

Dr Pratt

My tutor, Dr CLG Pratt, OBE, I had met while still at Bryanston, for he had interviewed me for a place at Christ's College, and made his personal impression at that time. At the interview, I had answered the traditional question upon my reading matter by mentioning Jerome K. Jerome's "Three Men in a Boat" and, in reply to the secondary question as to which character I preferred had keenly opted for one of the three participants in some detail. It was then that he declared his preference for the dog, Montmorency.

He was a striking person, particularly for his very direct manner in addressing undergraduates. His lectures on respiratory physiology were delivered extempore, while walking back and forth on the dais below us as we lined the auditorium of the Physiology Theatre. He was thoughtful and provocative, and notably different in his methods from others in a teaching staff that included such distinguished physiologists as Adrian, Matthews, and Rushton. It was said of Dr Pratt that his expertise in respiratory physiology had been at the service of HM Government during the war; there were hints of explosives and chemicals involved in the mysteries of weaponry, and of underwater research. It led to a wartime honour, of which he was most proud.

In college, he was Director of Studies for the medical students, and also gave us memorable supervisions in physiology. His method of teaching was welcomed by students first stumbling into this strange world of medicine, for it was direct, basic, and informal. In his role of Senior Tutor, his view of what constituted the best qualifications for admission to the college became notorious. He had a quick eye for personality. It was said that when a visiting schoolboy aspiring for a place at Christ's came across him in the courtyard, and asked the way to the Senior Tutor's Office, he was appropriately directed, and also advised that the Senior Tutor was a quite formidable person. By taking a back route, Dr Pratt was able to reach his office and be behind his desk when the candidate entered the room. The legend does not include an outcome, but my own experience suggests that if the student reacted adequately to the confrontation, his chance of a place there would have increased.

There were six of us who matriculated to start reading medicine at Christ's in 1950, and he knew us all well. At one point, he vouchsafed that two would become specialist consultants, but I never knew which two he meant. His faith in me was certainly greater than my own, for I found the initial impact of medicine quite demanding. I did not in fact react adversely when I first walked into the Dissecting Room of the Anatomy School and saw the rows of bodies laid out for us at the beginning of term, and I soon recognised that here was the most natural place for a medical student to be involved in the study of the structures which he expected one day to treat. On the other hand, I did not adopt the image of the typical medical student, casually cutting up cadavers and already *aufait* with the clinical world, for I did not see myself already as a doctor. Neither my own childhood, nor the independence of thought which Bryanston encouraged, gave me reason to aspire to the role of the traditional, affluent, and socially successful medical practitioner. I found it difficult enough to absorb much of the academic natural science subjects which constituted our course during the first year, while so much else seemed of importance to the personal view of medicine and social service which I was beginning to develop.

At the end of that year, I returned from the examinations one afternoon, certain that I had mismanaged my opportunities, and let down good people who had believed in me and given me support. For a moment, I contemplated the distance from the parapet outside the windows of our room to the ground, but my room companion Rex Howe was there, and instead we talked of the whole process of being a student and our inadequacies. He took a more mature and almost jovial view of it all, and I contented myself with awaiting the results. When they came, I was clearly not on the fast track, but could anticipate becoming a doctor if I worked hard enough.

Pre-occupied though I was with balancing medicine and the implications of being a committed Christian, nothing in my beliefs stopped me from playing rugby in a college team, drinking in the town, smoking late night cigarettes, and keeping engagements which necessitated entering the college at night, over some back wall, after the main gate was shut.

During my second year, George Kunzle founded the University Gymnastics Club and I became an active member. Gymnastics was not a widely recognised recreation in the early '50s but it formed part of the physical training in Dr Barnardo's Homes, particularly at the nautical training schools and at the William Baker Technical College; the Barnardo Boy Gym Teams were prominent in the public displays on fund-raising occasions. I was young when I first learned the groundwork, and had an early opportunity to use the parallel bars. At Bryanston, it was also a minor recreation, but it came into some prominence on Speech Day when a display was mounted for the entertainment of the parents. At Cambridge, George Kunzle, doubtless with a great family business behind him, was able to add financial support to his enthusiasm; the gymnasium at Fenners certainly became well equipped. It was there that I acquired a little ability on the rings and the horizontal high bar, but was never a spectacular performer on these. There were no inter-university competitions or possibility of obtaining a blue in gymnastics, but it was a past-time that I enjoyed.

I also joined the university and college Choral Societies, which gave me the opportunity to sing in concerts, including those in King's College Chapel, under the shrewd observation and baton of Boris Ord.

Despite my pre-occupations, I slowly began to see the relevance of our studies for the Natural Science Tripos, and my interest increased. The inclusion of comparative anatomy in the second year intrigued me, oddly enough, and I spent hours in the museum looking at the bones of other animals, detecting homologues, and considering their evolution. The collection of skulls in the Anatomy museum also fascinated me, and their evolution to encompass a brain capable of much more achievement than the passing of examinations, was somewhat consoling. I had not failed to notice the portrait of Charles Darwin in the Christ's College Hall, and the abundance of his books in the Library.

In the Department of Anatomy, Professor Harris, a small Welshman with a forthright and vivid approach to the topography of the body, was our ruling pedagogue, and all hubbub ceased when he walked into the Dissecting Room. He explained to us that the body was constructed very much like the college quadrangles in which we lived: supplies came to us from outside, waste was discharged towards the centre of the court, and services ran through the buildings. Dr James Millen was by then lecturing the third year students upon the anatomy of the brain and spinal cord, while Dr Gordon Wright supervised our brain dissection work and instilled some understanding of the clinical function of the nervous system. Our lectures in physiology had included brilliant demonstrations of the nerve impulse by Adrian himself.

It was the inclusion of pathology in our third year that began to make all the other subjects relevant, for it was clear that the specimens before us came from patients who had suffered disease, and the study of the tissues, both macroscopically and microscopically, brought together the basic Natural Sciences and clinical medicine. My attention to the effects of diseases upon the brain had been directed by Professor Dean, then well past the customary age for retirement, leaning over specimens on the table before him and talking of distinguished predecessors, who had given their names to various maladies, as though they were his undergraduate colleagues.

There were other reasons why my perspective changed during the third undergraduate year: I had met the person whom I later married, and we spent a lot of time in Cambridge together.

It was in my third year, too, that I accepted an invitation by the College Chaplain to address the Ridout Society - a body given to theological discussions and named after the Bishop who founded it. My subject was 'Christ's Healing Miracles' and I traced the accounts of these from the New Testament, through the Apocrypha and early Christian writers, up to the contributions from modern Christians such as Whitehead. It was a theme that began with an acceptance of the power of God to alter the course of diseased nature by miraculous intervention, and was related to the effect of faith on the response of an individual to disease. I was sufficiently interested in the mechanisms whereby thoughts and feelings acted through the brain to affect the rest of the body that, under the stress of one particular examination at the end of the year, I had the temerity to answer a question about the control of the pituitary gland by the brain.

I passed Natural Science Tripos at a second-class level, but needed higher marks in anatomy in order to continue to the MB BChir, which are the basic Cambridge degrees for qualification in Medicine. The qualifying examination in anatomy was on the morning following the May Ball, and I ventured to broach this unfortunate juxtaposition to Dr Pratt. He took the view that the May Ball at the end of my final year was a properly important engagement, so I danced the night through with the girl who had agreed to marry me, and went on from the breakfast at Grantchester to the Examination Hall in the university, donning my academic gown over my evening dress suit; it was many years before I wore such full academic robes in Cambridge again.

Dr Pratt's priorities had a perspective that I had learnt to value.

Anne

Praying in the quiet of the early morning at St Benet's I came to know my regular companions quite well. There was Canon A M Ramsay, from Durham, who was now in the University as the Regius Professor of Divinity. When he knelt, with bowed head and shoulders, and his great forehead between his praying hands, he was still tall. I knew by then that his fine intellect grappled with the eschatological side of the Church, and these were weighty matters. Nevertheless, whenever I met him going in or out of the church, he always greeted me with his smile and twinkling eyes. There was the thin lady with the scarf over her head, and the little lady with glasses, straggly grey hair, and quick darting movements. And there was the girl with the brown curly hair, whom I came to know best of them all. Sometimes she would come with the little darting lady, but often she was by herself, towards the front, on the left side, in the little Saxon church run by the Franciscans.

I knew she was associated with them in some way, for I had first met her in Northumberland, where she was one of a friendly community of Sisters who ran a Retreat House near Newcastle; they were bound together by vows within the Franciscan Third Order. Later, she was released from the vows, and lived with the little lady - Enid Welsford - to study Greek and other subjects, in preparation for becoming a student of theology.

We shared the same friends among a crowd of Christian students and ordinands associated with the Franciscans, and in this way became friends with each other. Enid Welsford's academic status, as an authority on the Romantic Poets and a don at Newnham, was disproportionate to her small stature. Her father had been a teacher at Harrow School, which made her no stranger to studious pursuits. She had succeeded at a time when Cambridge did not grant degrees to women, and the Newnham academics were considered blue-stockinged ladies. Her house on Grange Road had students other than Anne living there, and she welcomed me as a visitor. I believe she took glee in the romance budding beneath her roof. I made my visits to Grange Road in the quiet evening time, after dinner in Hall. I left the return to my own lodgings as late as the regulations permitted, peddling fast on my bicycle, with gown ballooned out in the breeze as I hurried to be back by 10 o'clock, when my conscientious landladies expected to lock their door.

Our friendship, with mutual interests in matters which concerned Christian students, seemed to meet the approval of our various other Christian friends, but in the early stages of the relationship there were times when I felt a wish to separate her from some of the budding ecclesiastics whom I could see were attracted to her. I thought that her upbringing, as a daughter of a Church of England vicar, placed her sympathies with those who were entering the Church. Gradually, I took her away from all this as I moved into the world of clinical practice and hospitals, and although we remained in touch with many of our friends as they climbed the heights of the Church of England and the religious life, we went a very different way together.

At Cambridge, our shared interests were initially centred on St Benet's and the Franciscans, who at that time still maintained their services for homeless men, and ran a large house for them just beyond the Castle Hill side of Cambridge. This was a rambling building with the friendly mustiness associated with the Anglo-Catholic movement. During term-time, they held meetings there for undergraduates to hear of Mission work, or to meet the Franciscan Brothers and attend discussions. Occasionally, I would join them in their chapel to say one of the various Offices of the Religious with which I was by then familiar.

However, our life together soon extended beyond the Franciscan Christian group. The college permitted women visitors until the closure of the gates at evening time, and there she joined us as we sang the advanced music of Constant Lambert, among other works, in the Choral Society. In addition, she attended meetings and social activities in college, through which she came to know the valued friends I had made there who were outside both my academic subjects and my religious concerns.

We shared interests in the music of the university also, and in those debates at the Union on political issues with which Christians had concern, for this was the time of the proposed Central African Federation, and the opposition to apartheid in both Africa and America. While our social life expanded, our knowledge of each other deepened; we became affectionate friends, but not impassioned lovers.

I knew a little of girls before I met Anne. There was the one in the village with whom I had played mothers and fathers as a child, and came to know a little more intimately during my later visits. My friendships and more affectionate relationships at Russell Cotes were with boys, and so were those that so marked me during my first two years at Bryanston. The friendship that I made there in my later years, with the girl from Cranborne Chase School, was a quiet one, marked by the occasional affectionate kiss and a real fondness, which I lost only slowly while she became a musician and I a doctor.

When I first lost my home base with the Johansens in Berkshire, my guardian, and a vicar in Reading whom he knew, arranged that I should stay with the family of a Scottish accountant, who was also a Freemason. I was introduced to a busy social life of teen-age boys and girls, as well as how to behave at a Freemason's Dinner. I became friends with a gentle and affectionate girl from the social circle there; I remember the warmth of her hand which I held in the cinema, and the long blue dress which she wore for a dance at Cambridge. By 1949, I had been representing Bryanston in athletics by running the mile, and it was necessary to do some training in the Christmas holiday for the AAA Schools Meeting at the White City Stadium. A student from a nearby family in Reading took me to the local track and I had my first lessons in serious physical training, which I never forgot. I achieved no great distinction at the White City, but became quite passionately attracted to my mentor's sister. She was slim, vivacious, had dark hair, and wore a red ball dress; I had difficulty in obtaining even one dance with her.

Those holidays acquainted me with students from affluent families, among whom I was seen as a promising youngster likely to obtain a place at a good university, but I had not grown up among all this, and did not really fit; I had no innate social ambitions, and was only slightly regretful when my holiday arrangements were changed, and I began to live in London.

It soon became clear that, as an undergraduate, I had to obtain some kind of job during the vacations to subsidise my housekeeping, for my scholarship provided just enough to pay my university fees and see me through each term-time. I began as a comptometer operator in the Accounts department of Wall's ice-cream factory. There I learnt the office gossip, and the wily ways of the office manager, who was reported to be a rabid communist, but looked relatively mild, with a small moustache and chocolate-brown suit around his red tie. In the next Christmas vacation, I wrapped parcels in Harrods, and saw what expensive hampers served as gifts for the wealthy, while I became expert in the folding of coloured paper and the tying of knots. Another student from Cambridge shared the job, and I was glad to find a fellow undergraduate as impecunious as I was. He told me a deal of why he was studying Foreign Languages, and I learnt to respect the relationships of our various European tongues, and the interest of philology and etymology.

It was as a waiter that I earned most of my holiday money and even acquired a little knowledge of how best to serve meals and drinks. My first waiting job was in a small residential club close to where I lodged in The Little Boltons, SW 10. I served breakfasts, lunches, and afternoon teas to members of the St. John's Ambulance Brigade, under the watchful eye of the Lady Manager, and with the jovial encouragement of the large Polish chef who officiated from behind the hot plate in his basement kitchen. I discussed my experience of working life in London with the two girls who shared the room next to mine in our lodgings. As the three of us lay on the soft carpet before the gas fire, drinking coffee and exchanging views, I was aware that while the fairer of the two was the more friendly to me, it was the other, a darker and more slight figure, to whom I was quite strongly attracted.

I learnt sufficient of the waiter's skills from that job to obtain a commis waiter post in the Piccadilly Hotel for the next summer holiday, by which time I was lodging out at the Barnardo's Girls Village Home, at Barkingside, in Essex. The formal black suit and bow tie which I had to wear was conspicuous on the Underground, and uncomfortably hot in the evenings as I hurried between the tables and the huge kitchen serving hatch; I soon learnt the advantages of the dicky, which I could don and doff at the hotel side entrance, where we were clocked in and out.

It was not only in the intricacies of the catering profession that my education at the Piccadilly Hotel progressed, for it was an international site of sociological enlightenment. The Head Chefs and Head Waiters were men of renown and idiosyncrasies; their affluence and the size of their London apartments were matters of rumour among the lower ranks. It was a multinational community with the foibles of males among males. The grass of Green Park, across from the hotel, was pleasant enough to lie on during the interval between serving lunch and dinner, but there was a need for vigilance to deter the sexual approaches of fellow waiters. The Englishman who befriended me while I learnt the job, proved to have been to a good boarding school, and had chosen the profession of waiting. He told me of his previous post as a ship's steward, and invited me to his comfortable flat for the afternoon. There I learnt more of his progress through the catering world and his interests. I soon sensed the likely nature of a more extensive friendship with him, and did not accept the invitation to return there in the evening, despite the tedium of the late night journey back to Barkingside on the Underground.

Having gained my employment by responding to a request for a commis waiter written on a blackboard in the side entrance of the hotel, and by referring to my previous experience as a waiter rather than my position as a student, I did not expand upon my term-time existence, or my vacation-time necessities. I held the view that an employee should prove worthy of the payment received, which was the prime reason for being there, and I did not expect any kind of deference to my position otherwise. Nevertheless, it was not for my skill as a waiter that I was promoted to the serving of drinks and suchlike in the large Entrance Lounge of the hotel. It was there that people met before taking lunch or dinner, or made a rendezvous to discuss professional or personal matters over a cocktail. In the afternoon, tea was served, accompanied by light music, and the same orchestra played throughout the evening until their rendering of the National Anthem marked the closure, around mid-night. In the main Dining Room a commis waiter was a fetcher, carrier, and server; he had no part in taking the order, nor did he handle money. My suitability for these last two duties caused my transferral to the lounge, ... became party to the whims of customers, and ... to their confidences.

It was there that a demure and well-dr... of uncertain age, with a crucifix on her ...ace, complimented me on my ability in serving her, and of obtaining for her a most particular brand of Turkish cigarettes. She finished by giving me not only a standard tip, which she knew I would hand in to the communal 'trunk', but also one for myself. I related this happy occurrence to Johnny, the experienced cockney who ran the bar in the corner of the Lounge. He had been around long enough to remember the time when the same lady was a very successful London hostess, and told me so; he knew that I was a student and expected to learn about people.

At Barkingside, Dr Barnardo's house was being used as a hostel for girls with various roles in the organisation. This resulted in my room for the vacations being the one on the ground floor previously used by the doctor for his study. Despite such segregation, I met girls to whom I was enough attracted to know what such relationships could mean. It was friendship, as much as any concept of physical fulfillment, that I appreciated, for I had by then accepted that the sexual side of love was the lesser part of a relationship primarily based on wider and deeper Christian concepts. A permanent partnership and children might follow friendship, and sharing of a life together; I thought of a sexual relationship in that context, rather than something to exploit beforehand. When the relationship with Anne developed within the Christian context that had become so much part of my life, it seemed not only a blessing, but also a wholesome growing-up; I moved away from what was becoming a precious male-orientated existence, and became a serious medical student.

My Barnardo background, having been confided to Brother Michael while I was a schoolboy, had never assumed any prominence among our friends, and it seemed quite natural to assume such a confidence with Anne; thus it became an accepted feature, which needed little discussion; it was not seen as a limitation, or as a matter for overt sympathy. Her parents must have taken a similar view, for they accepted me as a possible son-in-law warmly enough, without making further enquiry of my own family and prospects.

The disparity between my interests and my academic dedication as a third year undergraduate might have been significantly greater had not my friendship with Anne progressed to reach the stage of a formal proposal of marriage. It was a bold proposition from a homeless student, but I was able to mark its acceptance with a dainty ring, afforded from the jewellers shop in Petty Cury. More deliberation and parental advice might have countenanced a delay until I could produce a real income and a heavier ring, but it was a commitment that we were both happy to make to each other.

Our move to London was determined by the historical development of medical qualifications at the universities of Oxford and Cambridge. The Doctor of Medicine degree, which these universities have granted over some five centuries, has now become a distinguished academic rarity. Medical qualification is by graduation as Batchelor of Medicine and Surgery, in a process regulated by the General Medical Council of the country. These older universities fulfill the basic science requirements through a degree in Natural Sciences, but leave their medical students free to obtain the clinical training at a hospital of their own choice.

I chose to apply to Guy's Hospital, and appeared before a committee of physicians and surgeons there, well before I had taken the BA finals at Cambridge. It so happened that I had to stump up to the great table around which they sat, for I had one leg in plaster of Paris following a rugby injury, and this gave an immediate subject for discussion. After that I exchanged views with a distinguished physician upon the transitional architectural form of the Norman Galilee Chapel in Durham Cathedral, and then they granted me a place. It was a hospital that I had chosen not only because of its reputation for producing great physicians and surgeons, but also because I knew it served a relatively large part of adjacent residential London. I was likely to meet patients there with common conditions, rather than train entirely through highly specialised problems referred to the teaching hospital from a distance. I never regretted the choice.

Meanwhile, Anne had completed enough study of Greek, Latin, and other topics to apply to Kings College, London, to read theology. She having gained her place there, her anonymous patron agreed to continue her support, unperturbed by her acceptance of my proposal of marriage in the uncertain future. We became Londoners together. The university helped her obtain lodgings close to Russell Square, which put both the College and the University Library within walking distance, by our standards, for it was by walking that we got to know that part of London so well. I also managed to find lodgings, not too far away, in a boarding house that was on the south side of Argyle Square, from whence I could look across from my room and see the clock in the tower of St Pancras Station. It was easy enough to join the bustling crowd each morning to travel by Underground from adjacent King's Cross to London Bridge, and walk down the steps to Guy's Hospital nearby.

Central London in the 1950's was a lively place in which to live. We walked across the Kingsway to theatres to see the plays of TS Eliot, Rattigan, and Christopher Fry. We went to Covent Garden in the evening, to sit high up in the gods to hear the operas of Verdi, Wagner, and Bizet.

In the early morning, we went to see the Fruit Market at work around the Palladian porch of the church where current actors gathered, past actors were buried, and Eliza Doolittle sold flowers. It was little further to walk along the Strand and across the Thames to The Festival Hall, in its first years, to listen to orchestras for which its acoustics had been designed. All this we did at times and expense that students could just afford and we loved it.

The great churches of London were also within easy reach, and our interest in the Anglo-Catholic took us to All Saints Margaret Street for music and an incense-laden liturgy, or to a more homely St Alban's, Holborn, which seemed to gather parishioners, somehow, from the streets and alleys tucked around the Law Courts. Our own parish church was no more than the Hall which remained after St Bartholomew's, Gray's Inn Road, had been bombed to the ground during the Second World War. The parishioners were mostly students, like us, but from London House, nearby, which accommodated those from Commonwealth countries. The priest, a theologian teaching at King's in the Strand, had a comfortable flat in nearby Gray's Inn Court.

In the late evenings, I escorted Anne to her lodgings, mainly as a matter of courteous practise, for it was rare to see any violence in the streets. After a term or two, she moved to a room in a house near Corams Fields, not far from the Children's Hospital. One evening, as we passed a dark corner there, I ventured to remonstrate with a tall West Indian who was vociferously claiming a young lady who supposedly had promised to be his wife. He desisted without turning his attentions to me - fortunately.

I then thought it wise to move my lodgings a little closer to Anne's, and found a place in Doughty Street, which includes among its attractive early Victorian houses one previously occupied by Charles Dickens. In another, across the road, an elderly lady served me a glass of

Madeira in her basement sitting room, while she offered me a summerhouse in her back garden. I was grateful enough to accept at the time, for it was early autumn, and I did not know that the water supply, which came alongside the garden wall, would become frozen in the winter, and that the paraffin stove would cause the cream paint to fall in large flakes from the wooden ceiling and walls. Over another glass of Madeira, she explained that a previous occupant had been a retired mariner who had decorated the dwelling to the theme: "O all ye whales and little fishes, bless ye the Lord" which, after his departure, she had found intolerable, and over-painted it with cream. I did not stay long enough to reveal its former glory.

Anne and I shared a relationship at that time which was close, affectionate, and one of trust; her parents had committed her to my care. While she went each day to King's college in the Strand, to study theology, I went to Guy's and learnt about the care of patients. At the beginning, I was told of that balance of questioning and listening which obtained a good case history, and of the need to place the patient's complaint first. The history of the presenting complaint was to be followed by the personal and family histories, either or both of which might contain much of relevance, and a systematic enquiry of body functions ensured that nothing was missed. Examination of the patient consisted of inspection, palpation, percussion, and auscultation, using that modern symbol of the doctor – the stethoscope. The body systems were examined in turn: cardiovascular, respiratory, alimentary, genito-urinary, locomotor, and neurological. Thus, we made a thorough assessment of the patient before we considered any investigations, and we were encouraged to make a diagnosis at this stage, albeit a provisional one.

This clinical approach to a patient was a personal encounter, important to both participants. The privilege and responsibility of the participation was implied, from the beginning, but not expounded. I do not recollect being taught a specific code of conduct, and certainly was not presented with the need to prepare for the Hippocratic oath; it was more an apprenticeship, through which we learnt from the master physicians and surgeons of Thomas Guy's Hospital. I was glad to do so for I found their teachings closer to the care of patients than those of the Natural Scientists to whom I had listened at Cambridge.

At an early stage, our clinical teacher told us of the patient who lay on the couch, complaining that she could not walk, and she did indeed appear to be paralysed. A great physician saw her, and deemed the state to be one of hysteria. He then explained how this could be overcome, and demonstrated to his class the persuasion of the patient to walk, which she did, to the amazement of the audience. After leaving the clinic, she committed suicide by jumping off the nearby bridge. Thus, we learnt of the misuse of the power of the physician, and of the need to look for the problem that was behind many an initial presentation.

My own interest in the relationships between mind and body needed little encouragement, and I took it with me into the wards. In the successive three month appointments on both the medical and surgical sides we were identified with a particular firm of consultants, initially as clerks, and wrote out the full histories and findings for the patients designated to each of us by our chosen *gauleiter*. From the beginning, the difference in tempo and emphasis between the medical and surgical side was apparent, and I favoured the former.

Our clerkships included living in the hospital for the periods when our firm was on the rota for the admission of acutely ill patients, and so began the experience of sleepless nights punctuated with the crises of emergency assessments, resuscitations, and operations, between which we developed our medical student lives.

We had to face the sick, wounded, suffering, and dying patients with equanimity sufficient to care for them with clarity of judgement and efficiency of action. We did this variously: some would adopt a protective veneer that inclined to levity, while others felt the suffering within themselves, to a degree of moroseness, while, for some, morbid introspection would eventually turn them away from clinical medicine altogether. My disposition to care was strong, and my personal philosophy robust enough to take the responsibilities to patients seriously, without being overwhelmed: I continued to enjoy good companionship, both within the hospital and with Anne outside, and to play rugby without submerging my thoughts in the pub afterwards. I also sang in the United Hospital Choirs, under various conductors, one of whom took us to perform in the Albert Hall, which I regarded as a privilege. However, the course of the clinical medical student is arduous, and sometimes, after being in the hospital overnight for the firm's 'take-in' – the admissions of the acutely-ill patients – I would attend early morning Communion at the beautiful chapel in the forecourt, and welcome the time of reflection and peace. Occasionally, I would purposely get away from the hospital by walking out to London Bridge, which was close by. There I would lean on the parapet overlooking the 'Pool of London' and watch the loading and unloading of ships at Hay's Wharf. It was then that I thought of the life at sea which I was to have followed, and regretted the change.

Early in the second year of clinical studies, we took our turn as dressers in obstetrics and gynaecology, a speciality already then of importance in its own right. It was rewarding to go out on the district of the Borough and deliver babies onto newspaper spread before the blaring television. I also learnt more about women and their care, which was appropriate enough, for Anne and I had by then been engaged and almost living with each other long

115

enough to be certain about marriage, and the date was fixed.

On the 28th June 1955, in the quiet of the early morning, we gathered in the small church at Coxley village, in Somerset, for a Nuptial Mass. Anne's Father, as the vicar, conducted most of the service, but took up his role as father of the bride while a Franciscan friend joined us in Holy Matrimony before taking Holy Communion together. Another Franciscan preached a short homily before we went across to the nearby vicarage for a wedding breakfast. I then saw the considerable extent of the Somerset family that I had joined. My own support was in the form of my guardian, members of my Cuxham family, and Rex Howe, who was beside me for this undertaking, as he had been in our rooms during the first year at Cambridge. When I returned from honeymoon, halfway into our gynaecological dresser appointment, as a married man, I withstood quite well the knowing congratulations of consultant and colleagues.

Our clinical teachers were at their most didactic when giving their well-advertised lunchtime lectures. Dr David Stafford-Clark was a consultant of national renown from his radio programs as the 'Psychiatrist Today' and began a lecture on the anxiety state by describing the racing of his own pulse as he was delayed by the London traffic while in a taxi on his way from Harley Street to Guy's for the lecture. I had already read some of his popular Penguin paperback books on psychiatry, and knew that he wrote poems, and was a practising Christian. I learnt about the Guy's-Maudsley approach to the speciality in a three-month clerkship spent mostly at his outpatients, and was mildly encouraged when he illustrated his comments about expressions of personality by referring to the rose in the button-hole of my suit - picked that day on my way through the garden. I had already read an article of his in the Guy's Hospital gazette which extolled *panache*, shown in the choice of cars and clothes, for I remembered the word from Cyrano de Bergerac, performed during my time at Bryanston.

Nevertheless, it was in Dr Stafford-Clark's clinic that my attraction to psychiatry perished. He had introduced to us the case of a youngster with the condition called, at that time, Mongolism, and who had lived a limited but happy life until the day when his pet dog was run over. Thereafter he became so profoundly depressed that he responded to no one, was very inactive, would not eat, and was in serious danger of failing to survive. It was clear that his limitation of intellect enabled a simple enjoyment and happiness from his dog, but precluded an understanding of its demise, and any expression of grief. It was necessary to prescribe the only effective treatment available at that time, and a course of electro-convulsive therapy (ECT) was commenced. It was a dramatic example of behaviour determined by the organic structure of the brain, and commensurate with the Guys-Maudsley view of the organic nature of the major psychoses, and the concept that even the neuroses were often reactive, or precipitated by environmental or hormonal changes. Within these views the behavioural experiences of childhood, such as the frustration of either the need to love and be loved, or the desire to succeed in society – the hypothetical bases of Freudian or Adlerian psychology – were less important. More expediently, the long process of psychoanalysis was time-consuming and expensive as a way of practice, and even shorter-term behavioural or psychotherapy would come less easily to the busy practitioner than would a physical or pharmaceutical remedy. My belief in the value of self-analysis, with a view to re-adjusting behaviour and responses, remained as a personal concept, but was no longer so attractive as a basis for medical practice.

Russell Brock, the surgeon who was by then pioneering heart surgery at Guy's, gave a lecture prefaced with the remark: "Gentlemen, the heart is a pump, not a musical box" and continued with the exposition of assessing cardiac function by the use of methods which did not involve the stethoscope and audible minutiae. Sammy Wass was a blunt-spoken surgeon to whom I was appointed as a dresser. He treated the elderly lady from The Borough who was the first patient with bowel cancer for whom I cared in detail, as her medical student dresser, present before, during, and after her operation, so that I learnt the immensity of a surgical procedure early in my training. He also gave a clinical lecture in which, following a recent visit to the USA, he decried the tendency to initiate many expensive investigations without first taking a full history, and performing a detailed examination of the patient.

Professor Keith Simpson, the great forensic pathologist of that time, had already impressed me by the adroit manner in which he conducted post-mortem examinations of decomposed or exhumed corpses, while relating the grisly circumstances surrounding them. He made shrewd observations, which shed light on the most notorious cases, while intermittently dictating to his diligent secretary. His clinical lectures were sombre reminders of our future involvement with the law, one way or another, and from them I remembered always to convey my evidence to courts and lawyers in words as free of technicalities as possible.

Pathology, the study of disease as it affected body structures and processes, began to absorb me and to provide the objectivity whereby I could grapple with the serious study of medicine. After further appointments in medicine, a few of the major specialities, and as a senior dresser in surgery, my qualification as a doctor through a series of examinations that took place back in Cambridge, seemed relatively easy.

But not so the next year, during which I fulfilled the statuary requirements of working in hospital for a year ... to full registration, and also reached the decision to specialise. For this purpose I had to obtain and hold appropriate posts leading to higher examinations, while Anne kept our family life and various homes together. The first was a house in Croydon that a physiotherapist friend of Bunty Johansen asked me to take care of while she was on a long working visit to Canada. Having ceased being a scholarship-supported medical student when I had sat my final exams, I had taken employment in the Croydon branch of Walton's greengrocers, to keep us fed while we awaited the results. I was already an expert on the ripeness of melons when the news that I was a doctor reached me. We kept the house in Croydon while I did my year of pre-registration jobs 'on the House' at Guys, and we had Rachel, our first child, in the Croydon Hospital, and our son, Mark, followed some fifteen months later. We then lived in an end-of-the-terrace house containing the waiting room and surgery, near Epping Forest, while I did general practice at the weekends, and taught anatomy at Cambridge during the week. This double-time working was curtailed by the Professor of Anatomy, and we moved to Cambridge. I then had to rely on private supervision of medical students to support us, for the salary of a Demonstrator in Anatomy at Cambridge was so small as to be almost nominal. Following this I held a prolonged appointment in Casualty that provided valuable experience in surgery. It also enabled us to stay in Cambridge and to bring up our little family in a house adjacent to the grassy space of Parker's Piece.

When the obligation to National Service caught up with me, I took a short-term commission, in order to gain a better income and the opportunity to remain with my family; they accompanied me throughout my time as a military surgeon in Germany. For the short period that I served at the British Military Hospital in Rinteln we lived in Bueckeburg, and then we moved to live on the east side of Hannover, within easy reach of the woods, zoo, and the

Mittelland Kanal. Two of our daughters were born in BMH Hannover, and our life with the army flourished.

Our knowledge of Germany was expanded when a friend from Cambridge gave me an introduction to a widow and her family of four girls and a boy, who had recently escaped from East Germany to live in Hildesheim, not far from my post in Hannover. From them we learnt more of the sorrow of a divided Germany, and gained lifelong friends. Beyond the travels of my duty postings, we explored initially around the Weser, and then further away to the Hartz Mountains and the Rhine Valley, having developed a special code of conduct for travelling on the autobahns, which was introduced by a cheerful chorus as our Borgward Isabella traversed each Einfahrt. Through our life there as a family, and my extensive experience as a military surgeon, I gained an appreciation of Germany which was beyond the post war situation, and became the basis of a relationship which continued into my professional life.

Towards the end of my service, I obtained permission and completed the extensive documentation necessary for my family to accompany me on a posting as surgeon to the British Military Hospital in Berlin, at a time shortly after the infamous Wall had been built. The journey to and from the Eastern Sector involved passing through the East German and Russian checkpoints, in all of which our own Military Police briefed me. The East German guards looked at my documents and then saluted me, while I remained in the car; at the Russian checkpoint I had to leave the car, return their salute, and proceed to the little waiting room where I watched the Communist official slowly fingering through our documentation, while a sombre portrait of Khrushchev watched me. A military surgeon taking his wife and four children on a posting to Berlin seemed a matter for long consideration, during which I grew anxious for our welfare. Even the counting of heads in the car was a solemn problem to a cigarette-smoking guard, who could not agree the number with the documented list - until he spotted our fourth child, Jane, in a carry cot at the back – and gave a slight smile.

In the Western zone around the Military Hospital in Berlin, there was concern that there would be an invasion from across the Wall, and we undertook nighttime exercises to prepare us for this eventuality. These threats did not prevent us from visiting the Brandenburg Gate, near to which were wreaths on the ground marking the fate of those who had attempted to cross the Wall. We also took an authorised tour to East Berlin, to see the Opera House and Museums, for which I had to wear my uniform, and received friendly waves from East Berliners as we passed by in our bus. It was in the Dahlen Museum that our daughter Clare, by then mobile and somewhat elusive, slipped under the cordon around the exhibited Head of Nefertiti, and almost reached its glass case.

We returned from military service rich enough to buy a house, near Cambridge, where we lived while I made my second ascent of the specialist ladder to become a neurosurgeon. Family life, based in the little village of Melbourn, nearer to Royston than Cambridge, was relatively settled for Anne and the children, and it was there that Sarah, our fourth daughter, was born. I saw them for occasional evenings and some weekends, for I was back to House Officer duties, and resident in the hospital - limitations that were accepted as worthwhile, over some two years. A further year spent on research included normal home and family times among its attractions, and I was sufficiently free of clinical work to play in a local orchestra. The loss of so settled a life caused by my appointment to the London Hospital was disruptive, but accepted as inseparable from the advance into neurosurgery. We crowded into a flat situated in a sedate terrace owned by the Crown Estate Properties, overlooking Victoria Park, which enabled us to live in the relative splendour of Hackney, while I plied to and from the Whitechapel Road, day and night. Our younger children went to the local school, and the eldest travelled across London to a secondary school at Westminster; Anne and I were Londoners again, with a difference.

By then, Anne's father had become the Rector of Mells, in Somerset, where he had a most lovely house, to which we were often welcomed. I spent much of one holiday writing up my research work for the Cambridge Mastership of Surgery while the children played happily in the great garden there.

The decision to accept an offer of a post in the USA was primarily mine; Anne concurred, despite her wide family ties in the West of England, and the children viewed it as an exciting departure. We crossed the Atlantic in a cargo ship that ostensibly had room for twelve passengers, but accommodated thirteen by signing me on as a member of crew, but paying my own passage, and performing minimal medical duties. When we took a more northerly course near the possibility of icebergs, I thought of Anne and the children with concern during the night, as I watched them asleep in our cabin a few decks down. While at dinner one evening, an alarm bell sounded, and the engines were turned full speed astern to stop the ship. We had suddenly entered a fog bank, and the radar screen was turned on - only to display a vessel immediately ahead. In the quiet that ensued when the ship had stopped, we heard the voices from the smaller vessel as it crossed our bows; I knew then that I had taken my wife and family to a more perilous life, and they had come to be with me.

Our whole time in America, venturing deep into forests close to bears, camping on lakesides inhabited by snakes, sailing in a mostly homemade boat, meeting people who travelled with a gun in their truck, or just enduring the extremes of heat, tornadoes, severe frost, or snow, all emphasised our milder English existence.

My new colleagues, considerate of our English tastes, had found a brick-built house with mullioned windows, and this became our home. It was situated on the edge of the University Campus; close enough to know the academic community well. They proved to be an international community with wide tastes, situated in the midst of the Blue Grass State, with its great farms, horseracing, and borderline confederate history. We saw much of both campus and State, and developed a deep fondness of each. In the former, we joined a group that played early music, adding our recorders to rare instruments playing from hand written copies of even rarer music. We also joined the music in the Episcopalian church on the campus, and were invited, as a family group, to play in the churches of different denominations around the town. A young doctor sometimes joined us in these performances and also visited our home. She had grown up in the West, rode thoroughbred horses, lived on a farm, and talked of Colorado and Idaho Indians; I thought of her alongside of Huckleberry Finn.

Our children attended schools where integration of pupils from the locality around us was a pre-occupation. Rachel, our eldest daughter, found her place happily, while Mark, our son, remained orientated towards England. The younger girls grew up to American schooling, and flourished within it. Anne, too, found soul mates among the off-campus wives, with whom she could enjoy literary meetings. Both of us warmed to the unusual personality of a University Librarian whose husband had used a hand press in their house to print erudite tomes, and entertained such figures of the literary world as Aldous Huxley, first noticed outside as he peered for the house number, and Thomas Merton, who had taken leave from the Trappist monastery in the Kentucky countryside.

In the Appalachian Highlands, bordering Kentucky and West Virginia, there is a special community with Elizabethan origins, and much religious fervour, which I first came to know when the families awaited me outside the Operating Rooms, after I had treated one of their relatives. The Kentucky nurses, among whom I had good friends, helped to interpret the strange language, and enlighten me on the particular customs relating to illness, while I made an English explanation of the situation. I survived the exchanges, and learnt to appreciate their culture. Later, we visited their little settlements in the mountains. John Jacob Niles had collected many of their songs and came to our house one evening to sing some to us in his quaintly pitched voice. He accompanied himself on the Kentucky dulcimer, a hand made instrument related to the ancient viols. A friend very touchingly gave one to me when he knew we were returning to England. Despite our happy enjoyment of the people, the State, and many aspects of the country, it was I, as a neurosurgeon, who was the most doubtful settler of us all, and who brought us home again after a few years.

The decision to return was, again, primarily mine, with their concurrence, and I do not know how much of ourselves we left behind in that great country. Anne returned with our family of five fine children, and, on reaching the North of England, found us a home, while I tied up ends in Kentucky. Our family possessions were shattered by an accident in transit, but we collected the remnants around us, and began to re-settle our lives.

GM

The strands around which I have woven my professional life began almost fifty years ago, when I qualified as a doctor. A year of hospital work was required before full registration, and I had no doubt that I should try to obtain this at my teaching hospital. House jobs at Guys were competitively sought after, and I was fortunate not only to get my first three months there as a House Physician, but also to survive the attenuating process whereby only some of us continued on to the arduous three months as a Casualty Officer, followed by a six-month appointment on the surgical side. It was thus that I became the House Surgeon to Mr Grant Massie, known familiarly as 'GM', and at that time the Senior Surgeon at Guy's.

The process whereby I reached this point might well have begun when I held my appointments as a surgical dresser, for it was said that our consultant teachers assessed us *en passant*. An understanding of pathology, and recognition that I could manage practical procedures while a student, might well have equipped me for the surgical side. I had not sought to read the records and reports on me in the Medical School Office, nor had I ever discussed my background, for I thought our value was more a matter of present performance than past repute. Whatever apparent advantage the post-graduates from Oxford and Cambridge had when they joined the Guy's clinical course, it was no longer present at the stage of House appointments, and it appeared to be a matter of elimination whereby three full House Surgeons and the same number of House Physicians were appointed every six months. It was customary for the holders of these posts to be regarded as future Surgeons or Physicians.

By the time that I became a full House Surgeon the specialities of orthopaedic and cardiac surgery were well established in the hospital, and GM's interests were confined to those of abdominal surgery in general, and surgery of the biliary system in particular. However, the inclusion in his practice of patients whom I remember as having various limb conditions reflected his earlier interests. His overall stature was evidenced when the Dean of the Hospital injured his legs while at work on his farm, and opted to have his treatment under Grant Massie in the main men's surgical ward. I also recollect that it was he who excised a troublesome skin tumour from the back of an eminent neurologist colleague.

My respect and admiration for Grant Massie made my six months as his 'HS' the most formative of my life. He approached patients with gentleness and consideration, and operations with consummate care and dexterity; his knowledge was broad, from the days before specialisation in surgery, and he had at one time been a teacher and author in Surgical Anatomy. He also pursued problems in depth, and among these the decompression of the median nerve at the wrist to treat the Carpal Tunnel syndrome, which neurological physicians were beginning to diagnose, was an innovation. I had good reason to appreciate his expertise in re-forming the bile-duct following injury from previous operations when the striking coincidence of the Prime Minister of the country suffering from that particular condition with a severity sufficient to have serious political repercussions occurred at a time when GM was treating a patient with the same problem. The Prime Minister was transferred to America for expert treatment, while our patient, whose name and face I remember most clearly, had his scarred and distorted bile duct painstakingly re-fashioned by GM, and left hospital well recovered.

There was a degree of formality to being 'on the House'. As students we had used the basement cafeteria of the Medical College for our meals while on duty in the hospital, but the resident House staff had their table at the end of the oak-panelled Dining Room on the first floor, and left their white coats on the hooks outside. Our rooms were in the quadrangular remnant of the partly bombed college, and the Porters in the little office at the gateway called us, when we were wanted, using the titles of Dr for the House Physicians and Mr for the House Surgeons.

My inclination before qualifying was still towards medicine, and I had enjoyed my initial three months as an Assistant House Physician to Drs Hampson and Kauntze; the former had been a children's physician in the days before the speciality of paediatrics, and the latter was a polished physician with a large private practice specialising in cardiology. 'Hampy' was quietly thoughtful in his clinical approach, and gentle with patients; Ralph Kauntze was eloquent and precise; both wore morning dress when in the hospital, for they had already held early morning consultations at their private rooms in Harley Street, and would return there for further private practice later in the evening. It was Dr Kauntze who instructed me to reverse an attack of a particular form of palpitations in a patient by injecting a powerful drug into a vein while watching the reversal of the heart rhythm to normal on an electrocardiogram; it was an exciting procedure and I suppose interventionist enough to appeal to a budding surgeon. However, I took quite seriously the comment by my Medical Registrar that I would need to be more respectful to my immediate seniors when I went on the surgical side, and recognised that I was already by then somewhat independent and outspoken.

The three months in the Casualty Department were testing times; we had to diagnose and deal with whatever problem came across the threshold. One of my colleagues saw and treated an injured patient whose presentation was disguised by a degree of drunkenness. After leaving the hospital of his own accord the patient collapsed and died further along the road. Such events emphasised the responsibility of being the young doctor on duty at what was the hospital front door. The experience there not only prepared me for being a House Surgeon on duty for the admission of acutely ill or wounded patients who would require major surgical treatment, but also for being the front line doctor required to assess, diagnose and treat the acutely ill patient – a role fulfilled daily by the general practitioner.

When I had moved on to the House Surgeon post, and it was our turn to admit emergencies, I was called down to see a young man who had received a stab wound during some rioting following a 'Rock n Roll' concert near the 'Elephant and Castle' - a part of The Borough served by Guy's. The young man was about to die, and I just managed to obtain a chest X-ray, and the Catholic priest to give him the sacrament of Extreme Unction, before we took him to the operating theatre. The surgical registrar found what proved to be a stab wound which had penetrated the tip of the heart, and, since the emergency anaesthetist happened to be one already specialising in the management of patients undergoing open heart surgery, they worked well together. The repair was successfully done by using silk rather than catgut sutures, and just before closure, I, the assistant, took the opportunity to measure the distance from the skin entry to the cardiac wound.

The young man slowly recovered, and left hospital a few weeks later, which was not long before I was called to the Southwark Magistrates Court to give medical evidence in the case against his supposed assailant - a young man known to have been involved in the riots, and apprehended by the police, who then obtained a 'flick knife' from him. The weapon had been shown to me, and I mentioned that the blade was much shorter than the length of wound that I had measured at the operation. The case was pursued, and the barristers at the Southwark Court declared in public how the patient's heart had been 'taken out and repaired' by a remarkable operation at

Guy's Hospital. The hearing was transferred to the Old Bailey, and while the trial there was awaited, the police gathered evidence that there was another gang member, with a much longer knife, and he was still at large. On the day of the Old Bailey trial, it became apparent that the accused with the flick knife was a relatively new recruit to the gang, and the case against him was dropped in favour of extracting some kind of lead to the more dangerous assailant. As I walked away from the court, I felt some concern at being a key witness in such a matter.

A few months later I was again in the Southwark Police Station, having lost my wallet somewhere around London Bridge Station. The officer, about to write down the details of my loss, began by saying:

"It's Dr Brocklehurst, isn't it, sir?"

"Yes", I said, "But how do you know my name?"

"Oh! I remember you well from the McManohan case" he replied.

The wallet was returned to me.

It was not always by dramatic operations that patients were best treated. I admitted a man with very severe abdominal pain to our firm, and it seemed likely that he had some acute intestinal problem that warranted opening the abdomen. However, I had noted that his occupation was that of a painter and decorator, and knew that such people were prone to absorb enough lead from the paint to become poisoned, resulting in multiple complications such as lead colic. There was some evidence of lead poisoning apparent from examining his gums, and so we made this diagnosis, refrained from operating, but relieved his pain and watched closely. An hour or two later we had confirmation of lead poisoning from various blood tests, and we instituted special intravenous treatment with a 'chelating' agent which took up the lead and cured him. Grant Massie was much impressed and encouraged me to write up the case in

Guy's Hospital Reports; this was my first medical publication.

Expectations of me were high, for GM ran his firm in Guy's through the 'HS': he called in about patients from his rooms in Welbeck Street, or from his other hospital practice, in Putney, and when he arrived at Guy's it was the duty of the HS to meet him in the main colonnade, and to keep him in sight until he left. During the six months I spent most nights and week-ends looking after our surgical patients, excepting when GM invited me out: once to dinner in a restaurant off The Borough High Street, once to attend the Royal Military Tattoo at the White City, and once to see the most memorable performance of Berlioz's epic opera 'The Trojans'. There were also other recompenses for the long hours of work; he would sometimes invite the HS to assist him in operating on a private patient in Nuffield House, and I was most touched to find at the Medical College one evening the envelope addressed to me in his elegant handwriting, and containing a cheque for ten guineas – my first fee earned in this way.

Nor was it only just from GM and the Registrar that I learnt about the care of surgical patients; the men's surgical ward was under the care of a much respected Sister, who slept overnight in her office there when there were patients recovering from particularly large operations. She was experienced, skillful, and devoted. She was also so tactful that it was possible to perceive her intimations as we went round the patients together, and then to prescribe the appropriate treatment as the doctor in charge.

The patient with lead colic had made me reflect upon the control of intestinal contractions by the Autonomic Nervous System, and it was not long before I had to take note of the nervous system again as I assisted GM to perform sympathectomies to relieve vascular spasm and high blood pressure. This led me to wonder whether or not the underlying cause of gall bladder stasis could be dysfunction of the autonomic nervous control of the relevant sphincters. My interest in the role of the nervous system in abdominal conditions was followed by the thought that operations on the nervous system itself would have a delicacy and individuality, which would make them preferable to repetitive and so-called routine procedures in any of the other possible specialities, and I ventured to discuss my thoughts with GM. He advised me to visit one of his previous House Surgeons, Jim Hamilton, who was by then well on his way to becoming a neurosurgeon at the Guy's-Maudsley Unit in nearby Denmark Hill.

The visit consisted of joining him for a morning as he went about his work with the patients; I knew by then that he was a very well qualified Senior Registrar in the speciality. At the end of the morning, as we sat over a cup of tea, he said that if I was not interested in doing a great number of fast, curative, and money-earning operations, and was prepared for a long, demanding, and fastidious training and practice, I might consider neurosurgery. My decision to pursue the speciality was, therefore, based primarily upon interest in the nervous system; I hoped that I would be of service to patients, and I was likely to ask questions rather than pursue routines.

It was necessary first of all to qualify as a General Surgeon by obtaining the Fellowhip of the Royal College of Surgeons, and the Primary parts of the examination were in basic sciences, set at a level sufficiently high to pass relatively few, thereby excluding from surgery all but those with the diligence and application considered requisite. Anatomy was regarded as the most difficult to pass, and I was able to obtain a post as a Demonstrator in this subject back at Cambridge. The salary being inversely proportional to the privilege of the post, I needed to supplement it in order to support my wife and family. General Practitioners welcomed assistance, particularly if they were single-handed, and I joined one in Essex, near Epping Forest. My duties were to take surgeries, either in the GP's own house, where there was also a dispensary, or in the little terrace house beyond the railway, where we lived. I learnt to see patients in the context of their home lives and families, and the art of assessing their problems at the initial encounter. The pride in making a correct clinical diagnosis, albeit of a condition requiring immediate admission to hospital, was as great as the pleasure in caring for the whole patient and family.

Sometimes I would run the practice for the week end or longer, while my senior colleague had a break. Having not yet obtained a driving license, I did the rounds on a bicycle, and saw patients in their large and comfortable homes, up the hill towards the Forest, or in their friendly little terrace houses beyond the railway, and I enjoyed it. I came away one day from the home of two sisters, having been given a piece of a 90th birthday cake. A few days earlier, the elder of the two had seemed unlikely to reach this anniversary, on account of a serious infection. I had attended her morning and evening to give injections of penicillin, which saw her to rights again. As I walked away I wondered if there was any better form of being a doctor than this; I saw my course towards surgery an obligation by then, but would it be of such service?

After a month or two of this dual working arrangement the Professor of Anatomy advised me to move to Cambridge rather than commute from London, if I wished to concentrate on passing the Fellowship Primary examination, and this I did. The house that we rented, overlooking Parker's Piece, was central enough to use for supervising small groups of medical students in anatomy, and thereby adding to my meagre salary. My main work was in the Dissecting Room, and there I taught the students with considerable sympathy, having been in their position only four years previously. In doing this, I also gained such a detailed knowledge that I not only passed the Primary at the first attempt, but thereafter knew the topography of the human body sufficiently well to find my way around it wherever I was operating. It was necessary only to refresh our undergraduate knowledge of physiology and pathology to pass these subjects in the Primary easily enough, which reflects their importance relative to anatomy for the aspiring surgeon at that time.

It was at our home in Cambridge that I last saw Grant Massie; he was visiting the university as an Examiner, and he regaled us with an account of time spent at the Fitzwilliam Museum earlier in the afternoon, studying some pictures related to his own collection. As he took tea with us, I was again aware of his breadth of view, and his courteous consideration for me, his penultimate HS. He died not long after his retirement.

It was a very different side of Cambridge that I came to know during the year or so working as a Casualty Officer in Addenbrookes, when the hospital was on the old site, opposite the Fitzwilliam Museum. It was a necessary part of training for the Fellowship of the Royal College of Surgeons that I should be able to deal with casualties from accidents, and since the department served both the city and the surrounding countryside, I learnt well how to assess and care for injured patients. I was also able to help patients with emergencies that were as much social or emotional, as physical, and throughout those long hours of the night or weekends I came to know the less happy sides of both city and university.

One Sunday morning I spent an hour or two repairing a complicated wound of a farmer's forearm, sustained when working with his tractor. A brace of pheasants arrived two days later, and 1 had the duty of plucking and preparing them at home. On another occasion I was called in the small hours to suture up a bleeding tooth socket in a patient who had received dental treatment the previous day. To me it was a small service, but to him, a great relief following sleepless hours; he sent in a bottle of whisky for us.

It was while working there that I was requested to give evidence in court upon a patient who had received a cut across his forearm in some kind of brawl. I described the position and size of the cut in simple accurate terms, avoiding such words as 'laceration' and 'anterior aspect'. I was then asked: "Doctor, in your opinion, did the patient sustain bodily harm?"

Which reminded me that legal language is as extraordinary as medical terminology.

It was a department run entirely by two Senior House Officers who worked together during the week days, with one staying on to cover the alternate nights, to be rejoined by his colleague the following morning. In order to have the alternate week-end at home, we would each, in turn, stay on for the Friday night, do Saturday, and Sunday, including the nights, and be joined for the Monday together, before retiring home to sleep. It was important to be able to keep such long hours and remain clinically vigilant, and almost as important to remain courteous to patients and nurses; keeping some residual amiability for my family and friends was an extra achievement.

All experienced Nursing Staff in charge of an Accident and Emergency Department keep a list of regular visitors with unusual backgrounds. The practical value of being able to match a drunken or overdosed patient with the home or refuge customarily caring for them was valuable enough. Of even more value was the list of possible names and symptoms used by individuals with Baron von Muenchausen Syndrome, but it was still important to be sure each time that there was not a real wolf.

The final test was to remain calm and considerate for even the most overanxious or irritating patient when a queue of others with more obvious conditions was behind. In the six months or so that I held this post I was only once made aware that I had blundered: I told a young man, greatly concerned about having caught his finger in the door of his guest room, that it was idiotic to be requesting an X-ray when he could clearly move the digit so fully and painlessly. The letter of complaint, from a well known senior member of the university, stated that it was inappropriate to call his young guest an idiot.

More to the point, I learnt not only how to deal with both major and minor injuries, but also how to recognise and care for patients with conditions not curable by surgical procedures, but casualties nevertheless.

Military Surgeon

A motley collection of militarized doctors was of more concern to me than to the Sergeant Major. He had seen many through the parade ground of Aldershot Barracks and thought more of their medical ability than their marching, but I had been in Barnardos, where parading was routine, particularly in the Nautical Schools, and was embarrassed to see my companions unable to keep step or turn in the required direction. However, there was a deeper level to this military service as a Medical Officer, which I came across frequently enough in due course to provoke a personal stance that did not go unnoticed.

We had all been granted deferment of our National Service commitment while we qualified in medicine, a favour to us matched by the need of the Forces to ensure a supply of potential Medical Officers while call-up continued. I had been able to extend the Casualty Officer post in Cambridge sufficiently to complete the requisite surgical apprenticeship, and was working for Professor J S Mitchell in the Department of Radiotherapy when I appeared before the National Service Committee. The use of radioisotopes and brain scanning to investigate diseases of the nervous system was being developed by then, and Joe Mitchell had offered me a research post to pursue this. The Committee weighed this proposition against the diminishing need to supply the army with young doctors, and decided that they required me. Had they done otherwise, I would have missed both National Service and the surgical profession entirely, for the research would, almost certainly, have completely diverted me onto the academic side of medicine. More to the point, when I joined, the Army would employ me as a Surgeon rather than as a General Duties Medical Officer, provided that I took a three-year commission, and this I did. Immediate promotion to

Captain, married quarters in which to live with my f.
and surgical work in Military Hospitals within the B....sn
Military Zone of Germany was my gain, at the price of
deferring my entry into neurosurgery.

Our group completed the fortnight of basic
training, not without having been shown how to use a
gun, to protect our patients, if necessary, we were told. It
also was made clear that we were now serving in the
British Army, and could be ordered to go out and fight, if
necessary; we were officers – and then doctors. We took
the Sergeant Major to the pub to drown all retribution
before we then left on our various postings.

I began at Rinteln, up in the hills above the
Weser, where a German Military School had been
converted to a Hospital. It was a small and remarkably
peaceful place, particularly when covered with snow. Our
married quarters were in Bueckeburg, a few miles away,
and various well-known regiments were posted in
surrounding towns. It was from Minden that I admitted a
soldier with a stab wound to the chest, and inserted the
chest tube to drain off the blood that was compressing his
lung at a stage when he was still confused enough to walk
off down the ward. Later we had to do an open operation
to stop the bleeding. He recovered, and a few weeks later
was called up before a Courts Martial, accused of
assaulting civilians. I was also called, to give medical
evidence. It was my first attendance at such a function,
and I knew that I was supposed to wear the full formal
uniform of the Royal Army Medical Corps - the 'Number
Ones'. In fact, I appeared in 'Shirt Sleeve Order', for I had
been operating that morning and left the hospital too late
to call home and change. At the court, I explained the
reasons for my informal appearance to the resplendently
dressed Master of Ceremonies, who immediately said:
"That's quite alright, Doctor" and introduced me to the
President of the Court. I recognised a high-ranking
RAMC officer, fully attired in Number Ones, to my

137

consternation. I was soon into a detailed account of the injuries, and I noted that there was civilian representation of the soldier, and a civilian Judge Advocate controlling the legal exchanges. I was cross-examined on why we operated, in addition to inserting the chest drainage tube, and had to explain the technical problem of a half-severed intercostal artery. The following day the Commanding Officer of the BMH called me in and conveyed the Judge Advocate's compliments on the clarity of the medical evidence. In a further two days, he had the difficult task of relaying the reprimand from RAMC Headquarters to the 'Officer improperly dressed for a Courts Martial'.

I was next posted to Hannover, which had a large Military Hospital, taken over from the German army. There I learnt from my senior surgical officer how to pursue surgery in the army by the maintenance of diligence and high standards. We operated one night to relieve a young soldier's intestinal obstruction, and identified the cause as a congenital structural anomaly around which the bowel had formed a knot - a pathological mechanism sufficiently rare to justify a report. The resulting paper, which we published so long ago, in the British Journal of Surgery, still reads well and has some notable illustrations which I drew.

I then became intrigued by the number of troops being sent down to us from the Harz Mountains, with injuries sustained while skiing on the 'winter warfare' training course. I wrote a report on a series of these, and, by special request, was able to go up there as a participant, to see the conditions under which the injuries were sustained. During each day's arduous 'langlaufen' over the mountains, and at the evenings' 'après ski', I was treated as an infantry officer, under training, and I enjoyed it.

Nevertheless, a senior commander took me aside to ask for a medical opinion on a problem occurring following the overnight camping. Apparently, many infantry were falling unconscious to the ground just as they started the next day's trek. I was taken on an extraordinarily beautiful ski journey across the mountain slopes by moonlight to enter the camp just before dawn – and without being seriously challenged. A reveille call was sounded, and a tot of rum served all round, the men having just climbed out of their warm homemade igloos. They immediately proceeded to pull their heavy sledges uphill, out of the camp, and began to drop to the ground in significant numbers. I examined each, noting the slow pulses, the warm peripheries, and the rapid return of consciousness; clearly the rum had increased the pooling of blood in the warm peripheries, and the sudden demand by muscular contraction had further reduced the supply to the head, precipitating a syncope, or faint. Omission of the rum, and a more gradual mobilisation before heaving the sledges, solved the problem.

The problem of the number of ankle and leg injuries on the slopes was less easily solved. My report was about to be published when telephone calls came from the RAMC Headquarters, enquiring of the circumstances. The Brigadier Surgeon then appended a note to the report stating that the particular form of ankle binding was no longer in use.

A junior Surgeon, with a lot of experience in the assessment of trauma, and a little in speaking German, was a suitable person to respond to calls from German hospitals to which British personnel had been admitted. I would make an initial professional visit, in my civilian suit, and discuss management and transferral to our care. Difference both in clinical emphasis and financial interests could usually be settled, and the transferral arranged. When this failed, I would make the next visit in full uniform, supported by orders to transfer the patient, which usually succeeded. So strong was the German teaching that an injured brain should be treated by submitting the patient to prolonged bed rest that my removal of a bewildered soldier, who had tried to salute me when I found him tucked away in a corner bed after a minor head injury, was greatly deprecated by the nursing Sisters of the little hospital. They came out of the chapel and lined the corridor as we left and we had to run the gauntlet of their disapproving looks.

Many a transfer was made, in the relative discomfort of a military ambulance, from small hospitals tucked away in the hills above the Weser. Sometimes, we could call up a helicopter, most often from German military units, and these served us well, provided the command line was clear. I had already transferred a very ill soldier with multiple limb injuries from a little hospital, because circulatory failure was threatening his kidney function, and had him aboard a German helicopter and airborne, when I was asked by the pilot for orders. I knew we were expected at the University Clinic at Muenster, where they had one of the newly developed artificial kidneys, and we aimed for that city. Not knowing the precise whereabouts, I ordered a landing where I could see the Red Cross roof markings of military ambulances. This proved to be a depot, but a man there knew the way by road. He climbed aboard and directed us, as we flew above streets, taking turnings and crossing traffic lights, until we arrived at the Clinic. There we were expected, and before I had finished relating the history and biochemical data, the patient was attached to the dialysis machine. He did well, and was later transferred home to complete treatment.

Occasionally the American Forces supplied the helicopter. On arrival at the BMH the pilot would alight, and, with a proffered hand, introduce himself by a name that was already inscribed across his shirtfront. I was unused to such familiarity, and on the first occasion, got the patient and myself aboard the craft with some apprehension. Once aloft, we proceeded with a smooth efficiency and rapidly transferred the patient.

Furthermore, I was returned to the BMH accompanied by the equipment we had taken. The pilot dropped me off close to the hospital, after advising me how to avoid the current of the rotor blades. He was soon airborne again, and I was left in the middle of a field, sitting on the blankets. I mused on being a Military Surgeon. Thereafter, I always took American familiarity as an indication of serious commitment; I dubbed it formal informality.

From one small town there was an official complaint to our Commanding Officer because the helicopter had destroyed some of the flowers in the village square as it took off.

My duties in the hospital included daily ward-rounds, usually with one of the uniformed British nurses, ranked as a lieutenant or captain. Other nurses, in civilian uniforms, were more international. I came to know one of these who had noted my habit of humming The Pilgrim's Chorus as I walked around. She was travelling around Europe, and, having studied in Freiburg for a while, was now visiting Hannover. She had taken a post in the hospital before moving on again. We shared interests in music, travelling, and people, and became deep friends in the way that those working abroad so easily can. We met again in Muenchen Gladbach, when we attended a Mozart opera, and briefly in London, passing through. She then moved on to Switzerland, from whence she sent me some delicate flowers pressed into a letter. I did not see her again until many years later.

Senior officers in the RAMC tended to move away from patient care and towards military protocol; our Commanding Officer had insisted that the Duty Officer of the day should wear the heavy, leather Sam Brown belt. I protested that this was incompatible with clinical work, and the examination of patients, but had to obey orders. Shortly thereafter, he had to explain to me that an exchange between one of our officers and one from a

German Military Hospital in the Ost-Friesland had been arranged. He had resigned himself to sending me, as the officer proficient in both surgery and German, but would have preferred someone with a deeper commitment to the military life. I spent a few weeks there, seeing patients on the wards, and participating fully in the military surgery. I also operated, sharing a mutual delight with the operating theatre sister, as I made my requests for the instruments in my best German.

I had the odd sensation while there of waking up with my first thoughts in a different language from my own. We talked over Bier in their Officer's Mess, and after one long comparison of our different methods in the treatment of inguinal hernias, my German colleague nodded his head wisely and said: "Sind viele Weg nach Rom". I recognised that the British way was one of many, and used the phrase to head the published report of the exchange.

I was allowed to take leave and attend a short course in London before I sat the final FRCS. It is a qualification that I have always valued as the recognition of the profession of surgery, based upon both theory and clinical ability. The RAMC also recognised it, and graded me as a Surgical Specialist with the rank of Major.

From then onwards I was available to be posted anywhere else that such a specialist was required. The first position was in Muenster, and I had not been there long when the fourteen-year-old son of a Colonel sustained a supracondylar fracture of the femur from a sledging accident. I knew it as a rare injury, with the possibility of causing occlusion of the main blood vessels to the leg, and any form of reduction by manipulation was fraught with danger. I was able to achieve satisfactory splintage, and called the HQ Brigadier from the Opera House for advice. Evacuation to the UK was successfully undertaken.

My short posting to Berlin had no such clinical crises, but the knowledge that one day in three I was the Duty Surgeon for Spandau Prison was sobering, for it housed notorious War Criminals who were reaching the age when surgical emergencies might strike. Even more sobering was the knowledge that preparations had been made for the use of an underground operating theatre at the Sports Stadium, should there be a sudden invasion from the East German side. I spent one night awake and awaiting orders at the hospital while an exercise to simulate such an event took place, having been told that we were so close to the border that we would be rapidly overrun if it actually occurred.

I returned to Hannover in time to Captain the Rugby team for a season that involved a number of matches against local German sides. They tended to assail me, as much on account of my rank as on my scoring ability.

Overtures to extend my stay in the army did not fall on deaf ears, for I had enjoyed the lessons in military surgery, and recognised that we could be comfortable in interesting posts around the world; I might even have become ambitious to advance in rank - but my commitment to neurosurgery was paramount.

Walpole

There is both art and science in brain surgery, and while the latter is best learnt by diligent academic application, the former can only be acquired by apprenticeship. Of all the surgical crafts it, most particularly, requires the aspirant to start at the bottom and work upwards. Certainly, the tradition of neurosurgery that grew around the centres at Oxford, Cambridge, and The London Hospital was one of apprenticeship. Sir Hugh Cairns had learnt the speciality from Harvey Cushing, in America, where rigid discipline and fastidious technique had reduced the mortality of operating on the brain and spinal cord to a level somewhat nearer to other specialities. Cairns began to work in The London, and then accepted the invitation to start a unit at Oxford, supported by The Nuffield Foundation. He attracted trainees, including Joe Pennybacker, from the USA, and later, John Potter, Walpole Lewin, and John Gleave trained there, in the same tradition.

Cambridge developed its clinical Medical School well after Oxford, having eventually moved from the Old Addenbrooke's Hospital, opposite the Fitzwilliam Museum, where I had served much of my general surgical apprenticeship, to a new site, beside the GogMagog Hills at the edge of the city. A large Accident and Emergency Department was established first, backed by an orthopaedic service, and neurosurgery was introduced, with the initial emphasis on a service for head-injured patients. Walpole Lewin, who already had a national reputation in the management of head injuries, was appointed from Oxford, and the Cambridge Neurosurgical Unit developed under his aegis. In addition to innovating the major role of neurosurgery in the management of patients with head injuries, he enabled the establishment of medical neurology within the same building.

When I joined as a trainee in the early '60s, there was still quite an expanse of green hillside around us, and the city and university seemed far distant. Nevertheless, the Cambridge Neurosurgical Unit was an integral preliminary part of the large General Hospital which has subsequently developed there, and to that extent, it moved away from the splendid isolation which characterised some of the first generation neurosurgical units in the country – the 'ivory towers'. It also contained its own facilities for intensive care and paediatrics, both aspects of neurosurgery with which I became deeply involved, and these remained important in my concept of what a neurosurgical unit should do.

I made my interest in neurosurgery known to both Joe Pennybacker and Walpole Lewin, while I was still serving as a Military Surgeon, and it was the latter who accepted me. His role as Consultant Neurosurgeon to the Army facilitated my transferral back to Cambridge, for he recognised that the move from being a Surgical Specialist, with the rank of Major, to being a resident House Officer in Neurosurgery, greatly affected my income and family life.

I learnt first that the basis of good neurosurgical practice is a thorough history, followed by a detailed examination of the patient's Nervous System, with a view to identifying the site of the problem as exactly as possible on clinical findings, for all investigations of the brain and spinal cord at that time were invasive and potentially harmful. This skill was acquired by clerking the patients in, recording a history and examination, which included behaviour and intellectual function, the special senses, and detailed peripheral motor and sensory function. Special tests of the sense of smell, acuity of hearing, fields of vision, as well as orientation in time and space, speech content, comprehension, and calculation, were performed for each patient, and recorded in extensive notes that had to withstand presentations and discussions on ward

145

rounds conducted by Walpole with a high expectation. It was a discipline that deterred the faint-hearted and generated anxiety in most of the House staff. Withstood, it produced a life-long basis for successful clinical evaluation of patients with neurological problems, as well as documentation valuable to their future management and to clinical research. Sharing the medical residency with other doctors and nurses involved in the neurosurgical service provided sympathetic companionship, which I needed, and leaned on.

This stage of the apprenticeship required that I was fully involved with patients on the wards, and was banned from the operating theatre for that year. However, there were many invasive procedures undertaken in the ward, for both diagnosis and management, and I became proficient in these. On the day that a sudden complication caused cardiac arrest in a patient, I had no compunction in taking him quickly to the operating theatre, and opening the chest to massage the heart – the practice of that time – until it recovered. The incident was discussed on the next ward round, and Walpole, with a rueful smile, noted that I had found a way past the ban. His demanding posture, which deterred many an aspiring young doctor, had with it a sense of humour that encouraged me, and a few others.

Nights off, when I could join my family, were infrequent enough to value, and on one such I was driving my wife back into the city when a police car stopped me to point out that I was exceeding the speed limit through one of the villages. It was a small infringement, and when I declared my occupation, I was asked if I was on my way back to the hospital. I explained my working pattern and that I was spending valuable time off taking my wife to the theatre. I was summoned to defend myself in court, and my account was read aloud, to the interest of the Cambridge Daily News reporter. The next day I was called to Walpole's office:

"How is it that I have to read from the daily paper how hard my House Officer is working?" he asked, and then smiled. He acknowledged my application and enabled me to get an early rise in salary.

More importantly, I became the neurosurgical Registrar. It was then my role to be in the operating theatre as much as possible, and there I learned the special techniques whereby we could operate on the brain with precision. Detailed preparation of the operative site, a sufficient opening, minimal disturbance to adjacent structures, precise haemostasis, fastidious closure: features that meant success to the patient and neurosurgeon, but to others were a ritual.

The proximity of Fulbourne Hospital to Cambridge and the known effectiveness of certain procedures in the management of severely ill psychiatric patients, at a time when we had few successful psychotherapeutic drugs, combined to produce a small psychosurgical practice, which Walpole conducted. A young woman, totally disabled by religious obsessive compulsions so severe that she was too incapacitated to perform even the simplest activities of daily living, was admitted and prepared by me for elective resection of the cingulate gyrus. She appeared in theatre, anaesthetised, with her head fully shaved. It was then that Walpole spotted a very small pustule on her scalp, previously hidden by the hair, and declared that we could not continue with such an elective procedure with a risk of wound infection. The operation was postponed. Asked what we should tell the patient, he suggested to our anaesthetist that he should explain that we had undertaken the first stage of the procedure, which he did, as soon as she was awake. Straightaway, there was a notable absence of her compulsive behaviour, and this was so well maintained that the cingulectomy became unnecessary. My reservations over psychosurgery, therefore, occurred well before I read 'One flew over the

Cuckoo's Nest', but I also saw quite a few patients significantly helped by leucotomy during my training in Cambridge.

Walpole operated using sequences of terse commands, brusque, to the point of irritation, but the assistant remained patiently and persistently helpful, if he was to progress further in the speciality. As we moved towards closure, he would relax into charming good humour. We liked him, and learnt a lot. John Gleave was less formal, more innovative, and ready to expound the reasons for a particular procedure. He emulated Joe Pennybacker in many ways. He brought from Oxford the new techniques of operating within the brain by inserting probes with a three dimensional control – intracranial stereotaxy – which I learnt from him with great interest.

I was progressively entrusted with outlying commitments and was dispatched one day by Walpole to answer a call from Ely Hospital. There a young girl had become unconscious from acute hydrocephalus. I took her to the operating theatre, which was in the old part of the hospital that had previously been the chapel. I had reached the point of tapping the ventricles of the brain, to let off the pressure, as Walpole arrived to join me. In Cambridge the next day, on our ward round, he described the scene, as he entered the theatre, of seeing Brocklehurst silhouetted against the stained-glass window, engrossed in saving the patient. His sense of humour softened a disciplined and didactic manner. He was a small man, with a large personality that did much to develop neurosurgical practice at Cambridge before he extended it to the British Medical Association, the Royal College of Surgeons, and even HM Government. He shaped both principal and practice in my own pursuit of neurosurgery.

Mentors

Walpole Lewin stimulated my initial interest in spina bifida while I held my neurosurgical registrar post at Cambridge. The condition had a prevalence of three per thousand live births at that time. I had seen infants and children with the disfiguring open lesion of the spine, paralysis of the legs, and an enlarged head from associated hydrocephalus. He had noted that paediatric surgeons, particularly those in Sheffield, were operating on the open spinal lesion within a few hours of birth, and had reported some apparent improvement in the use of their legs. Inserting a tube with an incorporated valve to drain the excess fluid from the brain to the heart could treat the almost inevitable development of hydrocephalus. Such an enterprising approach was only possible in places with the facilities to undertake major neonatal surgery. Walpole inferred that, since spina bifida was a severe malformation of the nervous system, it should be attended to by neurosurgeons. He thought we should undertake formal neurological examination of the new-born infants, particularly with regard to the level of lower limb paralysis, both before and after closing the spinal lesion, and this became my first major research project.

The format was an assessment of the infant within a few hours of birth, discussion of the degree of disability, management, and probable outcome, with one or both parents, already close enough to being overwhelmed by so gross a malformation, and then the performance of a huge operation on a very small patient. We had accepted, by then, that early closure of these lesions gave the best chance of survival and wound healing. Our systematic study was designed to detect any reduction in the degree of paralysis. The majority developed hydrocephalus, which we treated by a shunting procedure as soon as it was clinically evident.

John Gleave introduced the Pudenz type of valve to Cambridge, replacing the more bulky Spitz-Holter valve used elsewhere. He developed the technique whereby we inserted the shunt tubing into the jugular vein, and then used it as an intravascular electrode, from which we could take cardiographic readings to identify when the tip had reached the atrium of the heart. This ensured a placement giving a maximal duration to the shunt function. Researching this, in conjunction with our colleagues who anaesthetised these tiny patients, was my second project. Both undertakings carried with them experience in the management of patients, parents, operations, and postoperative care, as well as the accurate collection of clinical data which I then reported, and published. The resulting papers added significantly to the care of these children and further stimulated my interest in the developmental pathology of the condition.

At the end of two years as Registrar, my clinical mentors supported me in an application for the Elmore Research Studentship at Cambridge University. In obtaining this, I entered the most interesting period of my neurosurgical training. To study the developmental pathology of the condition, I needed access to human embryos, and Professor JD Boyd, of the Department of Anatomy, a world authority on human development, gave me access to his material, and facilities in the department. I had already met him, and benefited from his advice, when I had worked in his department as a Demonstrator in Human Anatomy, for he had, by then, replaced the more topographically orientated Professor Harris of my undergraduate days. JD Boyd's book on human developmental anatomy was authoritative, and I found him warmly co-operative. I already knew most members of his department, and their help was encouraging. I was able not only to study in tremendous detail the structure of the whole spina bifida abnormality, but also the way in which the cerebrospinal fluid system within the human brain develops, with a view to relating this to the diagnosis and treatment of hydrocephalus.

On the clinical side, while continuing my interest in the spina bifida patients and their progress, I rejoined Professor Joe Mitchell, by then the Regius Professor of Physic at Cambridge University, and developed the technique of diagnosing hydrocephalus by the injection of a radioisotope, the movement of which could be followed on a newly developed gamma camera by scanning the patient. Joe Mitchell was primarily involved in the radiotherapy of tumours, and had impressed me a few years earlier by his lucid observations and bedside reflections on the behaviour of cancers. I shared an interest in German medicine with him, particularly after my time as a Military Surgeon in that country. He gave technical support to the hydrocephalus work, and was there when I presented my Cambridge Mastership of Surgery thesis successfully.

A year in which I had such widespread support while I pursued the study of an aspect of the Nervous System which interested me deeply, with the opportunity to spend hours in the University Library referring to ancient and modern tomes with tremendous enjoyment, or walking along the Backs reflecting on academic questions, showed me the privileges and pleasures of academic neurosurgery. The freedom from clinical emergencies, combined with ample time spent with my growing family, only enhanced its attractions.

I did not let the seeds planted by these distinguished mentors lie dormant for long.

The Whitechapel Road

My second period in the East End of London was almost as lonesome as the first, and much longer. Towards the end of my research year at Cambridge, Walpole Lewin intimated that I would be welcome to apply for a Readership at Edinburgh, but I thought that consolidation of my operating experience was more important, and applied for Senior Registrar posts in London. I obtained one in The London Hospital - at a time of change. Douglas Northfield, who had taken on the neurosurgery there from Hugh Cairns, had recently retired, but was around in the background, collecting material for his book, and the distinguished Russell Brain had just left the Neurological Department. Jack Crawford became the senior neurosurgeon, and Tom King, who had done much of his training at The London, was attracted back from Melbourne to the vacant consultant post. A number of the neurosurgical beds were a few miles away, at Brentwood - a wartime legacy to which Crawford was still committed.

I arrived, with a strong academic background, eager to gain more operative experience, but also to introduce new techniques and practices. Jack Crawford, a bluff person withal, was sufficiently friendly to invite me to dine with him at The Garrick Club. Both he and Tom King delegated clinical management and operations to me generously, commensurate with my seniority, and the radioisotope investigations for hydrocephalus were entirely left to me. The medical physicists disagreed with the dosage that we had developed at Cambridge, and I had to defend my view in a public discussion, and clear each individual case with the Medical Research Council, until the latter eventually endorsed my position.

My first year at The London was therefore busy enough, and became more so when Jack Crawford, unfortunately, quite suddenly died. Tom King, at that time establishing his own technique and reputation in the treatment of tumours around the brain stem – acoustic neuromas in particular - was a painstaking operator, and I learnt from him how to work carefully rather than speedily. When he became the sole consultant, it must have appeared opportune to centralise neurosurgery at The London before obtaining another colleague. During the interregnum, he covered the Brentwood side of the practice entirely, and I remained at The London, providing most of the cover there. In this way, I gained the operative experience that I had sought.

The London is the great hospital of the East End, including Stepney and the Barnardo headquarters, and I was both working and living a short distance from where Dr Barnardo himself had walked the streets, and where I had done the same as a fourteen year-old, preparing to go off to Bryanston. I was fond of it all: the barrows outside the hospital, the back streets, canals and parks, Dockland, the great river Thames, and the Rotherhithe tunnel and Greenwich footpath beneath it. Patients in the London had the language of the cockneys, the wisdom of the market place, and traditions that made clinical commitments on a Saturday seem slightly irreverent. I sometimes wondered how Barnardo would have viewed one of his boys being a doctor there.

Having written up my research work, I submitted it as a thesis on *The Pathogenesis of Spina Bifida* for the Cambridge Mastership of Surgery. For the accompanying clinical examination, conducted in academic gowns, I was shown a patient with a weak left ankle, and might have spent some time examining his peripheral nervous system and spine, had I not noticed a recent puncture wound with bruising on the right side of his neck. Clearly there had been a recent special x-ray investigation of the blood vessels of the right side of the brain, and I was able to diagnose a benign tumour of a certain type impinging on the brain to the right of the midline, where the motor

153

control of the left lower limb lies. I quite enjoyed the clinical side of the examination.

The thesis was marked by Professor Dorothy Russell, an eminent neuropathologist, and by Kenneth Till, the leader of paediatric neurosurgery at Great Ormond Street. They recommended the publication of certain sections of the work so specifically that I did this with alacrity. It was gratifying to me and my Cambridge mentors to have the higher degree, but I was then over-qualified, as well as over-worked, in my post at The London, and began to look elsewhere.

Once again, the academic side brought relief to the clinical intensity of neurosurgery, for I was presented with an opportunity of a travelling fellowship in America. It was arranged through some association between the Society of British Neurological Surgeons and one of the American neurosurgical societies, and consisted of attending a combined meeting of the two societies in New York, followed by a tour of the centres in Boston, Philadelphia, Lexington, and finally Washington, throughout which I gave lectures and presentations of my research work. At Boston I saw the paediatric neurosurgery in the Boston Children's Hospital, under Donald Matson, whose book on the subject I had read with great admiration. He kindly took me as his guest to The Country Club, which was a great privilege for such a relative junior. I also visited downtown Boston, to see the old colonial style houses, squares, and churches, and returned to my hotel late in the evening. When I told the door porter where I had walked he said: "Gee Doc, I sure am glad to see you back." Most of the other centres that I visited also concentrated on the neurosurgery of children, and the treatment of spina bifida and hydrocephalus was very relevant to them.

In the University of Kentucky at Lexington, I received a particularly warm welcome, and spent a day or two giving talks and seminars, and meeting all the staff of the neurosciences. I was quite surprised when, at the end of the visit, they asked me if I would like to join them. My response was politely negative, on the grounds that I was continuing my training in England, with a view to obtaining a consultant post there in due course - it had never occurred to me to change my country, nor had I ever considered such a possibility with my family.

A week or two after my return I received an honorarium of £80.00 from the American neurosurgeons. It was the first fee I had received for lecturing, and I used it to buy a silver flute from Ruddall Carte.

By this time, I had presented my work on spina bifida and hydrocephalus to various national and international meetings, through which senior neurosurgical colleagues came to know me. I sought advice from them on the likelihood of posts for which I was suited becoming available in England, and there were very few. I also visited Norman Guthkelch and the Combined Neurological Service that he had established at Hull, in Yorkshire, where he was hoping to appoint another consultant, but I recognised that his special interests were very similar to my own, and we would be in clinical and academic competition. I finally turned towards the offer from the USA as the one most likely to have the combination of clinical and academic neurosurgery in which I could participate.

Neurosurgeon Abroad

The view of New York from the penthouse of the Pan Am building was an impressive introduction to America. I was in a group of British neurosurgeons joining American colleagues for an international meeting, and had been taken straight from the JF Kennedy Airport to this elevated greeting party. I could see avenues and streets stretching away from below us, other skyscrapers nearby, and the magnificent bridges in the distance, as our hosts plied us with Martinis and made us welcome. The meeting, at The Biltmore Hotel, afforded opportunities to walk around Manhattan, and I soon became fond of the 'Big Apple'.

It was a spectacular introduction to a memorable trip on which I saw some of the best in paediatric neurosurgery, and the invitation from the neurosurgeons of the University of Kentucky to come and join them was encouraging, albeit a surprise. A few months later, when I wanted to move from the London, and saw no positions in England that could offer a good opportunity for both clinical and academic work, I took up the invitation, and was settled in Lexington soon thereafter.

For a while I felt at one with the previous generations of settlers from England: glad to face the challenges and prospects of this new land, and content to leave the old. Certainly, the academic position in a University Medical Centre was absorbing, for I found that research and teaching were the expected accompaniments of patient care, and I contributed to these with enthusiasm. I had the grand title of Assistant Professor in Neurosurgery, and all three of the neurosurgeons on the university staff had posts as Consultants to the Veterans Administration Hospital. I found the VA in some ways akin to working in the Health Service, since no fee-paying was involved, and I enjoyed my sessions there. I had a further and most particular role as a Consultant to the

Children's Hospital, which was run by the Shriner's Organisation. This post was clearly related to my previous experience with Spina Bifida patients, and was doubtless part of the plan to develop paediatric neurosurgery in Kentucky. I began the organisation of multidisciplinary clinics for these spina bifida children, and was soon quite intimately involved with the American charities primarily responsible for this kind of work.

The neurosurgical service worked closely with the neurological service - our offices and laboratories were in the same corridor. I came to know my colleagues in that department well, and enjoyed their academic and teaching roles. The Head of Neurology, Dr David B Clarke, was a distinguished physician, who had trained in leading American centres, but also knew the British centres well, and was an anglophile by practice and tradition. He was a senior colleague, and good friend. I was almost nonplussed, therefore, when I was asked to provide a confidential report on him. Apparently, even chairmen of speciality Divisions had to be assessed for renewal of contract every few years. I gradually learned that Uncle Sam had quite an element of Big Brother in him, and someone or another was checking us all. I made some friends among the younger doctors, and found that their conduct was not infrequently being looked at, and then advised upon, in a manner that I found disturbing.

There were aspects of my work in Kentucky about which I had misgivings from the outset. I was appointed an Assistant Professor in the university, but my patients had to be nominally under the care of my colleagues until I had the opportunity to prove to the State authorities that I was a properly qualified doctor. Cambridge, England, was recognised as an acceptable university at which to have trained, but I was expected to sit the Kentucky State Examination. My colleagues said it was merely a formality, but I took it seriously enough to revise subjects with which I was no longer familiar, and tried my best to answer correctly the lists of multiple-choice questions presented to me over three intensive days. When the results came out my high pass mark elicited compliments from the State authorities, and a degree of scepticism from me, for I knew that I had not answered all of the questions satisfactorily. Another odd formality was the Declaration that I would, in due course, apply for American citizenship. I was asked to sign this before an attorney at the beginning of my employment with the university, but nothing further was asked of me in that direction. It seemed as though my intention would be taken seriously if a probationary period proved satisfactory, for only then would American citizenship become relevant.

It was clear that I was not considered immediately to be a *bona fide* American neurosurgeon, and that I had first to contribute and prove myself. This was challenging rather than discouraging, and since my neurosurgical experience was already well up to that of my colleagues, I concentrated on the opportunities to teach, and to pursue my academic interests. I admired the thorough formal teaching that both medical students and residents in training for neurosurgery underwent, and I not only participated in this enthusiastically, but I also took the examinations in neurosurgery set by the Specialist Boards, and again passed with high marks.

Sitting at a table talking with American colleagues one day, I put forward a point and then said: "What do you think, Dr Brown?" "I'm so sorry, Dr Brocklehurst" he replied, "I was so intrigued by your way of speaking that I didn't listen to what you said". Perhaps it was my way of speaking which got me to the final in the Golden Apple Competition for best Teacher of the Year. The winner, however, spoke the most colloquial American of all the staff. The six-week course on neurosurgery for the clinical students soon fell to my lot, and I gave it standing beside the projected slides and captions. The Audio-Visual

Department asked to make videotapes of the series, to which I happily concurred, unaccustomed to such luxuries. Thereafter, I showed the tapes and remained in attendance on them. The multiple-choice test at the end was identical for each course, since all papers were handed in for marking. I was unavoidably absent for most of one course, and left it to the videos. That bunch of students obtained the best results in the examinations. I deduced that the content of my teaching was more important than my presence.

With a laboratory of my own, I was able to continue researching into the development of the cerebrospinal fluid (CSF) system of the brain, and the pathology and treatment of hydrocephalus. I was soon invited by other universities to give lectures and seminars on these topics, as a result of which I was offered a senior post at Toledo, Ohio. It was a university with a newly developed systematic approach to the teaching of medicine that I liked, but I declined the offer on the grounds that it was too early in my time at Kentucky, where I had been made so welcome.

Gunshot wounds, accidents from the driving of cars fast over rough countryside, and from other forms of violence, were common causes of admissions to the University Medical Centre. My clinical experience was widened, and we published papers and developed research into spinal injuries particularly. I began to develop extensive operations to correct and fix these lumbar spinal injuries, and to correct the deformed spines of the spina bifida patients. It was round the bed of a patient making a good recovery from one of these operations that the residents in training presented the procedure to Dr Charles Wilson, who had been the Chief of Neurosurgery at Kentucky, before he moved on to California. "I admire your courage, but not your judgement" he quipped; I was happy that he was just a

Visiting Professor doing early morning rounds with the residents.

My two fellow neurosurgeons and I attended some final meetings in Washington, with the expectation of receiving a large grant to expand this work, but it was given to another State that had recently experienced the striking down of one of its political leaders with a severe spinal injury. Another project of mine, to study the evolution of the CSF system, was highly commended, but not funded. However, I learnt a deal about applications for funding from these experiences, and did manage to obtain some smaller sums for my own research while there.

It was with the clinical side of the system at Kentucky that my misgivings grew, for it was quite clear that the residents were expected to care entirely for those patients nominally admitted under my name as the 'attending physician', unless there was a private or insurance fee involved, and that the operations on non-fee-paying patients were very much the residents' prerogative, in order that they could gain as much practical experience as possible during the relatively short time of their training. I had difficulty in thus delegating the care of patients admitted under my name, and was more inclined to impose my clinical involvement. Such interventions were said to jeopardise the appeal of the residency programme as one that provided plenty of practical experience for those in training. Weekly meetings, in which morbidity and mortality among the inpatients were discussed, in an academic context, were actually led by the residents, and in many ways were an admirable regulatory process, but I thought the role of Attending Staff, in relationship to patients' status, was not sufficiently questioned.

The fees that were, in fact, collected for patient care were put into the university coffers. From these funds, payments were made to the staff in the form of allowances for academic supplies and travelling, the level of which bore more relationship to academic seniority than to clinical work actually done. Nevertheless, I found them generous enough to enable me to purchase expensive books, and to travel great distances for conferences.

A particular concern of mine was the fact that the office of Coroner in the State was a political appointment, without the requirement of legal or medical expertise. They regarded the issuing of a death certificate more as a matter of the means whereby relatives could proceed with burial, than as a medical statement of the cause of death. There was little of the concern for the accuracy of the details entered by the physician on the certificate, which I had been taught in England as essential to its veracity. I had also been taught that whenever a patient's death was related to criminal acts, negligence, or just unknown, it was obligatory to report the death to the Coroner, who would then proceed to discharge his responsibility by investigating the situation, usually by authorising a post-mortem examination, and then having a certificate issued in due course. In the State of Kentucky, at that time, the physician in charge of the patient was obliged by statute to issue a signed Death Certificate, regardless of whether or not the cause and circumstances of the death were known, and this obligation was given priority over the Coroner's function in the investigation of the cause of death. The English practice had resulted in the performance of post-mortem examinations whenever there was clinical doubt, and this was a means of keeping clinicians and relatives fully informed, and of furthering medical education. In Kentucky, therefore, I persisted with my English practice, and refused to sign certificates where the cause of death was in any doubt. This led to my senior colleagues signing them on my behalf, while agreeing with me that the prevailing Coroner system was unsatisfactory. The number of such problems increased with time, as I persisted in withholding my acquiescence, and the situation became critical when this factor was combined with my difficulties in delegating clinical responsibility to the resident trainees.

My experiences of litigation in American neurosurgery were also quite discouraging. I gave evidence in two cases, both of which I thought were settled in the direction of maintaining the *status quo* of the current medical practice in the State.

My other major concern, as a neurosurgeon undertaking difficult and long procedures, and sometimes operating on very small infants, was the employment of nurse 'anaesthetists' to maintain the patient; the anaesthesiologist, a doctor, would oversee the nurse anaesthetists in a number of operating theatres. I had little confidence in this arrangement.

Persistence in maintaining my own position on these various related clinical matters was accompanied in time by some disillusionment over the position of academic neurosurgical practice as a whole, and this was not confined to me - I sensed unease among my colleagues. It finally became clear that I would not be continuing with the University of Kentucky, and I felt that I would rather return home than continue to strive unhappily with the American way of doing things. This was, after all, a time of great difficulty for the USA as a whole, as the Watergate affair unravelled. Slogans were to be seen on the cars: " America – love it or leave it."

Somewhere in America, I lost God. It was not a sudden event – one that might have led to re-thinking my personal philosophy and ethics somewhat earlier - but a gradual submergence of long held beliefs and practices. Around me, I saw cultural diversity and tolerance in personal and family relationships, which seemed the proper accompaniments to a great democratic country. Reciprocally, religious beliefs were less exclusive, less dogmatic, and less necessary; they did not determine the

162

prevalent ethos. That was more related to a patriotism induced in childhood, I thought, and nurtured thereafter by Uncle Sam; any serious immigrant would ultimately have to adopt it. There was also an intellectual factor: my research interests increasingly moved towards the evolution of a particular aspect of the brain – the cerebrospinal fluid (CSF) system – and the natural laws determining this process. This diminished the room for the supernatural, miraculous, or dogmatic, upon which my Christian beliefs and ethics had been based.

As a family, we continued to practise Christianity, and to attend the Episcopalian Church on the campus, but my personal philosophy gradually changed. The priority of caring for patients remained my foremost aim, while both teaching and research followed in support of this, but the need to face the economics of funding, and the necessary administration behind both clinical and academic practice, proved hard for me, for I had little natural political ability for either compromise or manipulation. Concepts and ideals remained very important, but, as I progressively discarded Christian ones for those more apparently relevant to my clinical and academic work, the integration of some aspects of loving fell apart. Mostly, service to others is close to the 'straitened' way of love of which Andre Gide wrote, but not always; caring for people is involvement, and involvement is not selfless.

I had by this time already begun to look back across the Atlantic, and had thought of being again in a nationalised health service, where there were plenty of hard-working patients requiring neurosurgical care, and no complications from fee-paying. Fortuitously, Norman Guthkelch wrote about this time to let me know that he would soon be looking for a further colleague at Hull, in the North of England. I decided that I should apply for this post, despite my earlier misgivings over the similarity in our special interests.

It was a privilege to have my American neurological colleague Dr David Clarke as one of my referees and he showed me the reference he had written – a customary practice in the USA. Among other things I read: "I have seen him work, and as an operating surgeon, he is quite good." I had to hope that other readers would also appreciate the American use of 'quite'.

Between Lands

Love's journey

On the night that we met, you were struck down and
lonely
By a blow which bereft you of him whom you loved.
And my heart knew no bounds as it turned to your
comfort, For in love we had started our journey along.
        I was there my beloved.

In the fields of between lands we wandered so slowly
Till we knew in our hearts love was calling us on.
And we climbed to the top of the mountain together
While below lay the world awatch for our fall.
        We were there my beloved.

We came down the hills alongside the valley
And we knew that through there lay the way of our love,
But the voices of many would have us not enter
For fear that our journey would take us away.
        They were there my beloved.

In the depths of the valley we came upon rockfalls;
We stumbled, we reached out, and then fell apart.
In the darkness I called you to turn round towards me,
Your hand touched my body to say that you loved.
        You were there my beloved.

In the light of the sun we came from the valley
To the place where our path lay again through the fields.
Beyond was the wood, then a house by the river,
And rest for the lovers who'd journeyed so far.
        You had gone my beloved.

Philosophy and Passion – a strange partnership.

The philosophy was pragmatic, not profound. I started to outline it in America, at a time when my beliefs were changing. Patient care was my primary commitment, and should remain so. Administration had to be next, in order to maintain the organisation and facilities for patient care in a speciality that made particular demands within the generality of medical practice. This aspect entailed application to paper work, meetings, and committees, with abilities to negotiate or compromise, which I lacked. Above all, it needed wile, which I never acquired. Research was the third component, and this seemed an innate necessity, both to the development of neurosurgery, and to me. Teaching was the fourth component - the normal accompaniment to a very specialized practice that my assistants were learning by apprenticeship. It included communication upon our neurosurgical practice in general, and publication of any results of research work. It was a philosophy of PARTS, the fifth letter standing for self evaluation – not only with regard to the relative proportions of the other four components, but also in relationship to colleagues, and personal conduct.

This philosophy contains what I consider to be the elements of medical practice in general, but many doctors will not emphasize research, or teaching, while some will lose contact with patients, and only indirectly be concerned with their care. All will probably agree that some administrative responsibility for their practice is essential, and many have allowed this to become their predominant concern, to the extent that some exchange patient care for politics. For some practitioners, research, or teaching, is their predominant role, their clinical training having led them finally in those directions; the ever-present demand of attention to patients is replaced by concern for grants, finance, and university politics. As for the fifth component - for all of us there must be an element of self-evaluation: the assessment of individual abilities and inclinations, personal ambitions, and priorities, including those of family life. For me, the order in which I spelt out this philosophy, not only to myself, but also in my practical filing system, was the order of my own priorities; the one closest to my personal ethos was the last.

The passion of which I must write was indeed profound, and very personal. Before it happened I had known a little of the feeling; it had touched some of my friendships, and some of my religious life; at times it had taken me forwards with a strength that had no hesitation, and no doubts. I had seen it lighten the eyes of mother and child, and of elderly couples.

When I met it so fully it pervaded my work, my thoughts, my whole being; it came through music, through a remark, through quite small happenings, and above all, through one person; it gave more significance to the big things that I undertook, and to small things like the Himalayan Balsam flowering beside the river in the countryside between us, where we often met; it gave me strength to continue when my practical philosophy failed; it persisted through all difficulties; it carried all the love I had known and not known; it lasted, and challenged my life.

I knew that a full response to this passion would certainly break up my family, and possibly threaten my professional life. It had been in my mind for many months before the night in which I paced to and fro' weighing it up. Against the certainty that breaking my marriage vows would hurt children whom I loved, was the passionate desire to love someone else, whatever the commitment. It was the belief that the passion would take me to a level of complete happiness and fidelity that tipped the balance. Such a fulfilling love would justify breaking up my family and dispensing with beliefs which had been proven inadequate. So I did.

Young woman with a large hat

"There's a young woman outside wearing a large hat who insists upon being seen by you, Mr Brocklehurst, and not by one of the registrars" said the nurse, who had not been running my outpatient clinic for very long.

"Is she tall, well-built, and outspoken?" I asked.

"Yes"

"Then I shall certainly see her".

I had known her from the time when the Children's Hospital had asked me to take over her care; she was one of the first children in the country to have a Spitz-Holter valve inserted for the treatment of hydrocephalus, and had done well as a child. While she was a teenager, however, control of the condition often failed, acutely, and we admitted her for emergency revisions of her shunt when her sight, and sometimes her life, were threatened. After multiple shunting procedures, I resorted to a special intracranial operation that I had developed while in America. This controlled the hydrocephalus, and she grew up into a young woman whom I would sometimes see around town, pursuing a very independent course, with considerable presence. She later made great contributions to the local community. Our outpatient exchanges were conducted in a bluff manner, to the re-assurance of us both.

My clinics had many patients with previously treated conditions that had threatened their life, limbs, or senses, and had required complex, lengthy procedures, followed by intensive nursing care. There were two other young women, both of whom had been initially admitted with serious brain haemorrhages caused by congenitally abnormal blood vessels. We undertook extensive operations, both to remove the clots, and to dissect away the abnormal vessels while preserving adjacent brain, which took many hours in each case. Both recovered, with some disability, and returned to active lives with a courage that I could only admire. I was invited to the wedding of one of them, only to await the bride's arrival - she had been smitten down as she was putting on her dress. I attended on her, and advised. The wedding was postponed for two hours, and she then appeared, radiantly happy as she was led into the church. She married and had a little family.

These, like so many others, I had known well as inpatients, and continued to see them long after. I knew their condition in detail and had good reason to recognise the particular nature of their disabilities, and any recurrence of their problems. The nurses also came to know them well during the years they ran my clinics – an unenviable task unless you could understand the people involved in the struggle of combatting disease of the most complex system of the human body.

Then there was the little girl to see. A month previously she had fallen over and hit her head while at home. Her doctor was called, and advised that she went to bed, but she was to be observed periodically. An hour or two later he was called again because she was unrousable. He telephoned me from the patient's home saying that she was deeply unconscious, and that he was bringing her into hospital. I was there to meet them, and could diagnose the condition immediately. A short time later, we had the child in the operating theatre, and removed a life-threatening blood clot from the brain. She recovered well enough to go home a few days later. I remember her because of the presenting circumstances which required such rapid diagnosis and operation that ancillary investigations and procedures were precluded; the clinically–based decisions were life saving. On review in the clinic, she was well, her hair was re-growing, and she would soon return to school. Patients like her, recovered from such serious conditions, were a joy to see, but passed from my memory much more rapidly than I did from theirs. A few I would hear from, over the years, and occasionally meet, grown older, but still well.

It had always been my practice to do as much as possible for patients with malignant brain tumours, despite the poor prognosis, for I took the view that a few extra months of life in these relatively young people was often worthwhile, provided that it was not accompanied by too severe a disability. The patients, followed up in a special clinic in conjunction with a radiotherapist colleague, who contributed much to their treatment, carried with them such concern and sadness, particularly when we observed deterioration, or had to convey the bad news following tests, that only our special nurse could comfort them. Our introduction of the laser and the use of phototherapy in these patients gave results that we analysed and published, but the memories of two young men with treated malignant brain tumours who lived to father children, and other young people who returned to gainful occupations for some years, mean more to me than our scientific results.

There were those who never reached my outpatient clinic, for one reason or another. One young man had a car crash on the way home from work, and within the area of a family practice that quickly got a doctor to the scene. He not only helped at the site, but got a message to us, so that we were in the A & E Department when they arrived. It was not long after my return from America, and I had established the role of the neurosurgeon in the assessment of patients with major head injuries: we listened to the account of the ambulance staff, and we looked at the patient as a whole, to detect the life-threatening problem, for the care of the brain involved the care of all other systems. In this case, we detected a very serious chest injury and immediately undertook the measures to relieve it. An hour or so later the nurses asked me to speak to his wife, who had been sent for. I was immediately struck by her personality, as she stood there with her children, and I explained what we had been able to do to save his life. He remained lightly unconscious, and I did not think his head injury was of great severity. Throughout the ensuing week or two, while we maintained intensive care, his conscious level was slow to improve, and it was then possible to deduce that during the most severe phase of the chest injury, while he was trapped in the car, his breathing had been so poor that the brain had been deprived of oxygen. He very gradually returned to a level at which he could talk, only to show no recognition of anyone around him, including his wife and family, and to behave in a manner which necessitated his transferral to a psychiatric centre for special long-term management. We had saved his life but not his personality, and the anguish of his wife and children was insurmountable.

There were others who, either rapidly, or after many hours of care, died on the ward from brain injury, or disease, in the prime of life, or as children, for many neurosurgical conditions are not limited to older patients

It was not unusual to complete the outpatient clinic and then go to the ward to see relatives, who had been given appointments to come and talk with me in the privacy of my office. There I would explain the patient's problem, simply, but not superficially, and what we could do or had done. So often, we were talking of severe disease, beyond our level of successful treatment, and likely to lead to disability or death. I felt for the relatives as much as I felt for the patient, and in some ways more, for I owed to the former the best of my objective judgement and management, for which detachment was necessary, whereas to the relatives, beyond imparting my knowledge and advice, I had only compassion and understanding to give, and I identified with them. At busy times, I would see three or more such families, after my clinic, and then go back to the wards or intensive care unit, to see patients and more relatives. Thereafter, a

171

feeling of emotional exhaustion ensued – I never became insensitive to this.

In the operating theatre, I introduced the disciplines and traditional techniques that I had learnt at Cambridge, and modified throughout the years in London and the USA.

Thirty years ago investigation of the intracranial contents entailed the injections of air or radio-opaque substances into the brain, or around it, which were invasive, relatively risky, and time-consuming procedures undertaken by the neurosurgeons in conjunction with their colleagues in neuro-radiology. The introduction of the computerised tomograph (CT) soon after I returned from the USA, followed by Magnetic Resonant Imaging (MRI) a few years later, enabled non-invasive brain scanning and the production of images with high diagnostic accuracy at any hour of the day or night. The neurosurgeon lost some of his facility for free-hand stereotactic manouevres and ability to read the radiological images, and increased his indebtedness to his colleagues in neuro-radiology. Their skilled assistance throughout my time, and personal friendship beyond it, was a privilege.

The increase in diagnostic accuracy and improved view of the operative site through the use of the operating microscope both enabled smaller wounds and produced better results for the patients. However, it was important not to lower the general standards of aseptic neurosurgical technique, and there was resistance to my demand for the removal of rings when 'scrubbing up' to operate. Discussions extended to letters in *The Lancet,* with personal convenience, sentimental issues, and unscientific studies ranged against rigidly held principles. I remained convinced that strict aseptic technique was preferable to anti-biotic coverage, if a hospital full of resistant microorganisms was to be avoided. The same principles applied to preparation of the operative site, preceded by an adequate skin shave, and were additionally important when we were inserting devices into the brain and circulation for the treatment of hydrocephalus.

On the other hand, I saw the advantages of the use of the laser as a neurosurgical instrument more precise than hand-held ones, or tissue aspirators. We had read some published results, and been to Graz, in Austria, to study the technique. After obtaining the instrument, with tremendous assistance from our surrounding community, we studied and published experiments to demonstrate its ability to make the controlled lesions necessary for operating deep within the brain, and then began to use it in our operating theatre. Its use in other branches of surgery was well established, but this was the introduction of its use for neurosurgery in this country. The early results were successful enough to reach the news head lines, and patients were referred from elsewhere in the UK and abroad for the treatment of difficult conditions of the brain and spine. We accepted patients for whom we had possible treatment, when referred by their doctors or other specialists, and tried to avoid desperate self-referrals, and those patients with advanced difficult conditions which we had little chance of improving. More importantly, we recorded the conditions and procedures with accurate notes which we subsequently analysed and collated, rather than base our decisions on the more spectacular cases.

We further developed the use of the laser in conjunction with a form of dynamic phototherapy for malignant brain tumours, and analysed the results in a randomised controlled trial.

The procedure whereby a lesion was placed in the depths of the brain using a probe directed by a three-dimensional guide calculated from radiographs of the brain, which I had so painstakingly learnt at Cambridge under John Gleave's expert tuition, was used primarily for

173

the treatment of the shaking in Parkinson's disease. The development of successful drug treatment for the majority of patients with this condition relegated the use of the stereotactic procedure to just a few centres, but the use of the modern brain scanners for stereotactic guidance facilitated our development of this same technique for obtaining specimens from deep within the brain to aid diagnosis and treatment. This replaced the free-hand passage of biopsy instruments, and improved the results.

Endoscopic, or 'keyhole' neurosurgery, was much more difficult; the surgeon cannot see his way through the brain with such an instrument in the same way that he can elsewhere in the body. Only within the central cavities - the ventricles - that are filled with clear cerebrospinal fluid, and other similar small spaces around the brain, is direct visualisation possible. Nevertheless, after attending meetings and courses on the use of the neuroendoscope, we developed it in the later years of my practice. It did not provide the alternative way of treating hydrocephalus that I had hoped, and it proved of limited use.

One case sadly revealed its limitations - and my own. A teenage youngster had presented with an urgent threat to his vision, and probably his life, from a rare tumour in the centre of the brain. At an open operation, using the operating microscope, and a technique that I had developed and published, I could not get access to the tumour without great risk to important mental functions, but we relieved the pressure, and saved his vision. I used the endoscope to do a further operation in order to establish the diagnosis, remove the tumour, if possible, and obtain permanent relief. I made the free-hand passage of the instrument, but miscalculated the direction in trying to balance the deep position of the tumour against the deformities from the previous procedures. The depth of the insertion was appropriate for the position of the tumour, but the direction passed closely by the ventricle and on to important areas of the brain, which caused a serious left-sided paralysis. This was apparent as soon as the youngster recovered, and I recorded the details of the procedure and complication at the time, and informed the patient and parents. I also asked my younger colleagues if they considered I was too old to be doing complex neurosurgery, but they thought not, and I continued my clinical service, including night and call duty, until full retirement age.

The patient made quite a good functional recovery, but remained weak on his left side. The case came to court a few years later, by which time the incident was too far removed to discuss sensibly any details of the procedure not recorded in my notes. The two days of medico legal exchanges before the case was settled out of court proved to be the most tortuous of my considerable experience. I did not discover if the misjudgment of a surgeon could be defended, but I did confirm my impression that the adversarial legal process is the most expensive and least satisfactory method of compensating a patient for unexpected disability following a neurosurgical procedure.

We also looked carefully at the results of our use of the endoscope, as we had with our other innovations, and learnt therefrom. The patient was compensated, but remained without a confirmed diagnosis, and at risk from further problems.

After my unhappiness with the arrangements for neuroanesthesia in the University of Kentucky it was encouraging to have a neuroanesthetist of great experience join me at the time of my appointment to Hull. He remained until our respective retirements, providing a highly skilful service to our patients throughout procedures that were life-threatening, and of long duration - often many hours. Always the patient would awake quickly enough to provide an early chance to assess their post-operative neurological state before they were returned to our intensive care unit. He proved also to be a much valued friend with whom I shared an interest in playing early music, and running long distances.

Our skilled nurses in the theatre were able to assist with complex procedures and innovatory techniques, as well as maintain the strict routine of traditional neurosurgery; the very low incidence of complications from infections was mostly due to their thoroughness.

It was my custom before each operation, as we prepared the unconscious patient, to relate the clinical history and findings, and to put the various radiographs and investigations on the screen. This enabled us to check the side and site of the problem before making the incision. Thereafter, we were undertaking what was so often a highly demanding and elaborate procedure, during which there was no room for other considerations than the task in hand. Only towards the end could we lessen the intensity, and think about assessing the patient as the anaesthetic wore off.

The service we provided for the surrounding population of about one and a half million consisted of taking calls and emergency admissions at any time of the day and night. One of the two consultants had always to be available, and we covered emergencies week and week about; a week on call meant seven days and nights continuously. Night calls occurred frequently, and required an alert, appropriate answer, followed by the ability either to go back to sleep again, or to get up, and travel in to see the patient, arrange investigations, and sometimes, to operate, regardless of the commitments of the previous and coming day.

It was at nights that I appreciated so greatly the introduction and progressive improvement of the brain scanners. I also valued the diligent and willing radiographers who operated them so well, and became my true friends.

Again, it was an emergency in a child too urgent to allow scanning that haunts my memory. He had been some weeks in a paediatric ward for treatment under the label of NAI – 'non accidental injury', which, in this case, meant that his initial state of unconsciousness was deemed to be due to intentional injury by an adult. On the night that I was called, he had become more deeply unconscious; we operated quickly, and evacuated a large abscess from the brain, to our surprise, for there was no clear relationship to the postulated trauma. The child made a poor recovery, and the case against the accused proceeded. In court the prosecution dramatically emphasised the postulated mechanism of injury, with little evidence to support it, and the defence related the unexpected abscess to the admission history and findings in retrospect, to suggest the mechanism was one of infection from the outset. The jury took a while to conclude that the accused was guilty of injuring the child.

Afterwards, I reflected that a medical opinion is normally based upon the history, examination, and investigations – as in the customary discipline of diagnosis. While there is both art and science in the balance between exact measurements and clinical observations, their reduction or rejection by prior assumptions is bold – and hazardous. Belief in the medical history, as obtained from the patient or relatives, is axiomatic; its disbelief is presumptuous. When combined with postulates incorporating a moral stance, and further reduction of the diagnostic discipline, the opinion is more missionary than medical. In court, the so-termed experts' opinions are subjected to both the emphases of the barristers, and perceptions of the jury; detached objectivity is therefore essential. In the case of this child the adversarial process of the law had extended to the expertise, I thought, and it was difficult to reach the truth.

Confronting the law is a not uncommon experience for a neurosurgeon, for we work in a speciality involving a high level of morbidity and mortality; the legal repercussions are manifold, and our involvement inevitable. I fully accepted my role as a witness to fact when I had been involved in the patient's treatment, and preferred to limit my expertise to this; I avoided, wherever possible, appearing in court as an expert in cases involving patients who had not been under my care, lucrative employment though it was.

I also had claims against me, as the surgeon responsible for procedures that went wrong. None were so gross as operations on the wrong side, or the wrong place, but sometimes the level of a spinal procedure proved difficult to define because of variations in anatomical and radiological interpretation. Sometimes, a procedure delegated to an assistant judged to be experienced enough to perform it, did not give the expected result, or produced an unforeseen complication; it was my responsibility for failing to get the correct balance between the need for trainee experience, and its supervision, when the expediency of running a busy service precluded my presence.

The increased number of neurosurgeons, and consequent reduction in working hours and clinical load, which has occurred in the last year or two, may well reduce the rate of complications, but continuity of care will require a lot of co-operation between individuals.

As an active neurosurgeon, I always held the greatest reverence for all human structures, particularly those of the nervous system, and my method of operating was slow and careful; I liked neatness, but not speed. Patients more disabled after their procedures than I had anticipated are painful memories, but the balance of operative skill against the complexity of neuropathology was never entirely predictable. I had more than a modicum of success, but did not have infallibility.

Anecdotes or analyses? How best to account for the life work of any kind of doctor? The anecdote belongs to memory and smacks of legendary brain surgery, whereas analysis is our research duty, and forms the basis of scientific neurosurgery. I have found motivation in both. A final analysis can hardly evaluate the individual lives that have been saved, some to live fully, and some to remain seriously disabled.

Furthermore, the economics of neurosurgery are difficult to calculate. Expensive resources are required, and many procedures are only possible within a service such as the NHS. Consequently, the majority of patients and neurosurgeons, and the NHS, are not involved in the high finance of private practice.

Objective analysis is difficult. Our own reported scientific series measured outcome in such simple terms as survival, and only occasionally have we looked at quality of life in measurable terms. Undoubtedly the modern scanning devices have so greatly improved diagnosis that operative procedures have either been rendered unnecessary, or have moved progressively towards increased accuracy and decreased exposure. My impression is one of improved outcome, and increased expectation.

Donations and Dockers

I came into neurosurgery at a time when it was emerging from being practised in isolated units to being placed within or close to general hospitals, from whence the majority of patients were referred. Furthermore, the founders of the unit at Cambridge had foreseen the increasing importance of the Intensive Care Unit, inseparable from the surgical treatment of our patients, and had developed the facilities for this alongside the neurosurgical wards. This was already the practice when I was in the University of Kentucky Medical Centre, so that I returned to Hull convinced that these advances in the speciality should be established and maintained there. In order to do this it was necessary to obtain and safeguard the facilities, and this involved the administrative role, which I placed next in priority to clinical care, but found so irksome.

Recognising the particularly expensive equipment required for neurosurgery, I instigated our own fund-raising efforts that proved successful by virtue of the remarkable support from the Humberside population. I went out to many clubs, pubs, and institutions to talk of the work, and to receive donations accompanied by speeches and the attention of the press. Most generous of all was the response of the dockworkers when they heard that I wished to introduce the laser to neurosurgery in Hull. At a general meeting called to accept a pay rise and return to work after a period of industrial action, the Shop Stewards called for a ten-pound donation from each docker, which was unanimously agreed, and in a short time we received the first twenty thousand pounds towards the device. Soon, we were able to begin the pioneering work with the laser technique. Through my subsequent involvement in meetings and courses, I made many good friends in the dock industry and National Dock Labour Board, before it became privatised.

Our fund-raising activities were formalised into a Registered Charity with four trustees: a solicitor, an accountant, a hospital administrator, and myself, as the clinician and neurosurgeon involved in raising the funds. It was called The Brocklehurst Neurosurgical Fund for no better reason than this was what the earliest donors called it, and put the same on their cheques. The trustees ensured its accounting, its priorities for dispensing, and its independence of the Health Authority. From then onwards many thousands of pounds were donated, duly acknowledged, accounted for, and used for specific items of equipment, including the specialised apparatus whereby we could use three dimensional images from the newly-developed brain scanners to guide our intracranial surgical procedures. We also supported a series of research projects into head-injuries, hydrocephalus, laser anti-cancer techniques, and brain tumours.

These various activities brought the recent advances in care to our practice in Hull relatively early, with benefits primarily to the patients, but also to our own national and international standing as a Combined Neurosciences Service - the term for the unit that I inherited, and was happy to maintain.

It was with this support that we were able to establish intensive care facilities on the neurosurgical ward before general units of this sort were available, and integration with our anaesthetist colleagues demanded considerable administrative skill. Initially it consisted of approaching hospital administrators who had often themselves worked their way through the various departments, and retained their faith in it as a public service run out of public funds, entirely for the care of patients. Much could be done with the direct co-operation of the Hospital Secretary, who was always nearby, but as these individuals were replaced by Administrators in offices further away, and the Consultants were gradually moulded into committees, guided by regulations, I had to pursue a form of administration for which I had not been trained. When I brought to the committees propositions for furthering patient care based upon the principles and practice of neurosurgery, my vehemence was met with more detached negotiating techniques, but I remained mostly successful. At one point, the Health Authority made direct provision for a major item of operating theatre equipment entirely on the grounds that we had already demonstrated prowess in the use of such a device.

The very specialised requirements of neurosurgery competed with other more general services, which treated a greater number of patients, using less time, and less expensive equipment; the discussions on the priorities of requests, therefore, had to be presented with good factual information. From the beginning I promoted the accuracy of the clinical records and patient statistics for this, as well as for other more academic purposes, and to this end developed computerised records and coding systems, mostly in my own time. I was an early participant in national systems of clinical coding, for which the government was responsible. In all of these systems the problem of measuring the qualitative outcome of patient care, in addition to recording the numbers treated, was never really solved in a manner that permitted valid comparisons between specialities and administrative areas, particularly when the latter changed with the constant forming and re-forming of the various Health Authorities.

When our local Health Authorities became powerful bodies with Chief Executives and Medical Directors, I was already a senior clinician. The exercise of power distant from clinical responsibility appeared to me iconoclastic – the doctors had to be brought down. On one occasion, I took a call from a distant military establishment, asking me to re-admit a patient whom we had recently treated by an emergency operation. We had relieved a very malignant condition affecting his lower spine, to his immediate benefit, and I knew him well. I also knew that we had nothing further to offer in our own unit, and suggested they should try to admit the soldier to a bed where palliative treatment could be undertaken. In essence, I had a duty to keep neurosurgical beds available for the next emergency patient, for whom we might be able to do a great deal. The army authorities complained of my decision in a formal letter. The Chief Executive, with less experience of the Army, and considerably less knowledge of how best to run an emergency neurosurgical service than I had, organised an exchange between me and the Medical Director, a colleague junior to me. This, I gathered afterwards, constituted a reprimand sufficient to include in an apology that he sent to the Army. The whole exchange reminded me of my military service, and the preference for protocol over patients.

Nevertheless, we continued to run a neurosurgical service that never turned away a true neurosurgical emergency, even for patients from a considerable distance, and had a waiting list of only a few patients, extending over a few weeks. It is fortunate that upwardly mobile Executives soon move on.

Administrative roles at a central Departmental or Regional level I fulfilled dutifully, but, excepting the Department of Health's meetings on Medical Records and Coding, and the Committee for Examining Post Operative Deaths (CEPOD), with little enthusiasm. In some, my role was merely to advise on appointments, and when I opposed the candidate favoured by the local incumbents, on what I thought were proper grounds, I was seriously unpopular.

I never held, or sought to hold office in the administration of our own Society of British Neurological Surgeons, but I attended its meetings diligently, in the UK and abroad, and, when I did so, quite often gave a paper on our most recent work. They were refreshing occasions of exchanges with colleagues, whom I knew and appreciated. When the meetings became more complex, and concerned with administrative and political problems, my enthusiasm waned.

Evolutionary Studies

My academic research work at Hull began with a three-year laboratory research programme to study the Evolution of the Cerebrospinal Fluid (CSF) System of the Brain, supported by quite a substantial government grant from the Medical Research Council that I had managed to bring to the local university.

In the second year of the project, the university attempted to delay the publication of some important findings, on the grounds that the evidence was insecure. Since the topic was one in which I had considerably more expertise than any of the committee members involved in the interference, both clinicians and academic scientists, I progressed from the communication already given at a national meeting, to publication in an international journal, with complete justification, I considered. Subsequent observations elucidated the earlier ones, and I had no compunction in including these; they concerned a basic observation of crucial significance to the study, and I considered its communication to be more important than the misgivings of the local university.

However, the whole exchange proved so different from all my previous experience of university-based research work, and so difficult to contend with while pursuing full-time clinical neurosurgery, that I did not attempt to extend the project, or start another one in the same circumstances. My refusal to renew the work was probably a disadvantage for a university endeavouring to promote its medical science interests at the time.

The study provided the basis of a PhD thesis for my research assistant, and for my own Cambridge Doctorate of Medicine, as well as some valuable publications. I also had the honour of communicating the results at the Royal College of Surgeons, in the form of an Arris and Gale lecture, subsequently published in the Journal of the R C S.

My research had changed to clinical observations on hydrocephalus when I appeared before a gathering of senior neurosurgeons considering me for a professorial appointment. One of them, whom I already knew, suggested that my research interests were in a relatively unimportant aspect of neurosurgery, and I took that amiss.

When I turned to the introduction of laser techniques to neurosurgery in Hull, there was a spate of publicity and the referral of patients to us from elsewhere in the country and abroad. It was clear to me that the real measure of such techniques would be their objective clinical recording and comparison with our results and others, using earlier techniques, in the tradition of the great surgeon, John Hunter. Assembling the clinical information that measured the results of laser neurosurgical technique was, therefore, my next research activity. The opportunity to balance the advantages against the disadvantages of this expensive and difficult form of instrumentation was made widely available through our communications to national and international meetings. Not all of the communications have reached major scientific journals, the editors of which have many pragmatic considerations, but in 1992, I had the honour of presenting this work as an Hunterian Lecture to the Royal College of Surgeons.

Valued Apprentices

Our neurosurgical unit had no formal academic status but I undertook teaching nevertheless. Sessions for didactic teaching were fitted into the weekly timetable for visiting students and Registrars in training, and in the clinical form on ward rounds, in outpatient clinics, and in the operating theatre. It was a role that I enjoyed. From my experience in the University of Kentucky, I was already familiar with the use of modern audio-visual aids when I returned to England, and I naturally added these to the more conventional bedside and clinical teaching methods.

More importantly, I had daily and nightly opportunities to teach the younger doctors who aspired to become neurosurgeons. They were our most valued apprentices, from many parts of the world, who, while learning, gave me such support and assistance that I remained forever appreciative and came to know them as young colleagues. They are now widely scattered, and I hope have taken some of the pride and practice of good neurosurgery with them.

In addition to communicating the results of our laboratory and clinical research work through publications and medical meetings, I also contributed to nursing organisations through meetings and journals, and to lay audiences, often in the course of raising funds. It seemed useful to replace some of the mystique associated with brain surgery by straightforward factual accounts.

In 1992, I had an invitation to talk to the sixth form of Ampleforth College, having had opportunities of treating one or two patients from this distinguished Catholic School. I was asked to present the brain as part of a Lenten series, which had started with the body, and was to finish with the soul. It was a great privilege, and since I had been specifically informed that it was to be an address, without audio-visual aids, I accounted for the structure in a manner which made its organicity clear, by both word and gesture, and its theological implications in no doubt: '*Cognito ergo sum* – I think, therefore I am'. I presented the brain as the organ of thought. The monks and sixth formers in attendance were an appreciative audience, and some came to talk to me afterwards. The Abbot most kindly sent me an honorarium that I spent on Iris Murdoch's *Metaphysics as a Guide to Morals.*

In the last decade of my practice the formal teaching methods were being replaced by those available through personal computers 'on line', which are more acceptable to trainees striving to meet the particular objectives of accreditation in their speciality. I restricted myself, therefore, to the residual roles of clinical teaching, by participation and example, which, I believe, are still important to the acquirement of the neurosurgical art.

Wherein lies merit

I took the opportunity while holding the academic post in America to put together my work on spina bifida in the form of a book, *Spina Bifida for the Clinician,* which met with approval. I also developed and published a new operative technique for the treatment of hydrocephalus, which was described as an important innovation, and included this with other observations, in an entry to the Society of British Neurological Surgeons, for the Sir Hugh Cairns Essay, which I was fortunate enough to win. It was a particular privilege to present the essay as a paper to the SBNS soon after my return to this country. However, when my senior colleague at Hull presented the proof of a very interesting paper which he had written for publication in the journal *Brain,* as an 'answer to the Cairns Essay prize', I should have recognised the rivalry which I had anticipated when I was considering joining him.

I had returned from America experienced, well qualified, and with their practice of free discussion, regardless of seniority. Unfortunately, I also lacked deference, it seemed, for, not long after my return, the same colleague, supported by others, held a meeting to advise me of their disapproval. When I appeared oblivious, their concern took more covert forms, and thereafter it was difficult to distinguish anxiety from animosity, or reproach from rivalry; of acrimony there was no doubt. My apparent criticism, during academic and administrative discussions, of those senior to me, and my maintenance of close interest and clinical control of patients under my care, even when on holiday, as though not trusting my colleagues, were two of the expressed concerns. However, neither the Health Authority involved, nor those outside the local professional situation, considered there was sufficient in these concerns to alter my clinical role, and the affair ran its course, while I continued to maintain my full clinical service.

Nevertheless, I felt threatened enough to take professional legal and medical advice, and was re-assured by objective expert opinions that my behaviour was independent, somewhat frank and outspoken, but not untoward. The official re-assurances, which answered the concerns, did little to restore confidence in my ability to manage inter-professional relationships satisfactorily for the future.

Among the many thoughts that arose from this experience, the choice between staying where I was or moving once more was foremost, and I sought the advice of a wise and distinguished civil servant whom I had come to know from my time on the Council for Barnardos. He advised that I should continue the work that I had started and 'lie low, and keep your powder dry'. The senior colleague principally involved in the reaction to my behaviour, left the country soon afterwards, and others, who had also been involved, offered me personal re-assurance of their altruism in the matter.

The rifts that had occurred were covered subsequently by the practice of customary professional courtesy, in which I made some progress. I have had few real friends among local medical colleagues since that time, and I never recovered fully from the initial antagonism that I had provoked.

The establishment of the neurosciences in general, and neurosurgical practice in particular, was then very much a matter for my own industry. I began by ensuring that the particular consultant in whose ability, training, and qualifications I had the highest confidence, was appointed to share with me the responsibility for providing the neurosurgical care for our surrounding population. To provide such a service one of the two consultants had to be on emergency call duty at all times, and we took the responsibility week and week about, as an addition to our long working days. Hence, it was usual for the care of patients to take so many hours of the day and night that the arduous side of the work became its predominant aspect. I once expressed a regret over this situation, and my listener, for whom I had great affection and respect, replied that my work was of the nature that few could do, and was therefore a privilege. I took the rejoinder to heart.

The expectation of patients and families, which was not commonly high when I first started in the speciality, increased, and they were understandably more demanding. As a result of training in Cambridge and the London, and particularly from my American experience, I talked as freely and honestly to patients and relatives as I could, commensurate with their understanding of the brain and nervous system - and our own - for I wished whatever authority I conveyed to be based on knowledge rather than aloof dogma. Such candour was uncommon at the time and our speciality had an aura of mystery that set it apart. Gradually, however, patients' agreement to neurosurgical procedures, like that to others, developed to become 'informed consent' with its legal repercussions, but there remained always the balance between the comprehensions of the patient and those of the surgeon.

Similarly, I recognised early that my nursing colleagues, who were so closely involved from moment to moment in the care of the patients upon whom I had operated, knew not only their clinical state in more detail than I, but also their personal and family particulars. I thought it important not only to listen to their observations, but also to appreciate their particular role, and to bring to it ready and frank explanation of the rationale of the operations and clinical practice.

In 1992, aged 60, when I had completed some twenty years of this highly specialised and demanding clinical service, had delivered a Hunterian Lecture to the Royal College of Surgeons on 'The Laser in

Neurosurgery', and organised an international meeting of neurosurgeons in Hull, my local colleagues put my name forward for a Distinction Award, but the proposition never got past the Regional Committee.

The Merit Award process was a matter towards which my ambivalence had been so prolonged that disappointment was hardly justified. It was originally designed in 1948 to ensure the continued participation of clinicians in the National Health Service, as opposed to more lucrative private practice, by the possibility of gaining a financial award for meritorious service. The questions have always been: wherein lies true merit? and How best is it detected? I had heard of the system when I was a Senior Registrar, but knew only vaguely its manner of working when I took up my consultant post. It was generally thought that neurosurgeons qualified early for the awards because of the rarity of their speciality, and the intensity of their clinical service.

I balanced my disdain for a system that I considered too dependent upon the local medical social network, against the undoubted honour that was as welcome to my pride as the increased income was to my bank manager. I also benefited from unsolicited national support in the process, which was an important component in the earlier years when local support was uncertain. In time I was progressed through the first two stages and the award process itself became more democratic and overt, at both the local and national level, as it emerged from its archaic origins. The Regional Committee, however, retained maximal anonymity and power, with minimal public accountability.

There seemed little doubt as to my level of distinction in 1992, according to a number of knowledgeable people whom I later consulted over the situation. Perhaps the animosity, which I had aroused so long ago, still prevailed, and had reached the all-important Regional level. It was a level at which my membership of various national and regional administrative committees had been uncomfortably fulfilled during my later years, and I had done little to alter my independent views, or my reputation. It is easy enough for such an Awards Committee to say that one aspect of a candidate's medical practice is short of being meritorious, as I wrote in the outline of my own pragmatic philosophy; but clandestine deliberations do not have to be justified in public.

Our position as a 'high prestige' speciality enhanced by our own fund-raising and academic efforts seemed to have jeopardised rather than promoted my standing among local medical colleagues, and I continued to disregard this personal aspect of my professional practice to my disadvantage. The actual day-to-day (and often night-to night) service remained deeply enjoyable and rewarding, however, for I greatly liked the patients, their families, and the communities from whence they came.

Clinical experience such as this, in which the proximity of distress and joy, and death and recovery, are so very real, leaves little room for dogmatic beliefs based on miracles. I have increasingly accepted whatever I understand of the natural laws governing the behaviour of the nervous system, as the determinant of my endeavours, and of the outcome for the patient. It was always my hope that in pursuing clinical science in this wholehearted manner, there would be some concurrence between good professional ethics and the Christian form of loving service from which I started, but sometimes I have fallen short in both.

In the last year or two, particularly since the terrorist bombing of the Twin Towers, I have been more definite about my detachment from the dogma of Christian belief, for it is from irrational belief that fanaticism arises, but the forms through which I have for a long while tried to hold together being loved and loving, remain with me.

HBB

Some years ago a gentle person, who cared, rescued me from a life of launderettes and take-away meals. I was living alone, having broken up a family, irrevocably it seemed. Walking along one day, I saw a woman with lovely dark hair, and wanted to touch it; I was really alone. Among the loose ends and fragments, there was my work, and I had turned to it so fully that I became more engrossed than ever. The pragmatic philosophy behind it carried me through, and in time outstripped the passion, leaving me with a deep yearning. I had lost a family, and a home; I moved from place to place, in relative impecunity, and I thought of myself – that neglected component of my philosophy. It was then that I first wrote at some length about my life, which made poor reading, but good therapy. I turned to music rather than to drink, and I started long distance running - it had been part of my youth, and I had remained active and fit as a student, and even as an over-worked doctor. It was a solace to be out running alone, but also a challenge; stubbornness and stamina were important then, and have remained so. In time, when I reached marathon distances, it became a method of raising funds for our work. Two colleagues, who have proven lifelong friends, supported me in these efforts, and our running has persisted.

The loving person, who joined me at my loneliest time, did so after we first had dinner together. We both needed close friendships. We shared our time, our rooms, our resources, our work, and our affections. In time, we shared a house in the Old Town, and an enjoyment of the great river that was nearby. Professionally, we progressed, independently, but with understanding for each other. We shared a commitment to caring. Our professions had been pursued by hard work, from simple beginnings, and we shared a disregard for social status.

We have both derived our ethics from Christianity, by different routes, and have come through turbulent times. I have found someone able to share both the occasions of professional achievement, and the times of personal failure. We have travelled the world in pursuit of professional interests and personal enjoyment. Most of all, we have filled a lovely home by the river with a family of two boys who have grown through a settled childhood, and are making their own lives. We have found a love in caring for our own, as well as in caring for others.

The promise that I made to the journalists so many years back has become a pre-occupation only recently. Origins and upbringing were not an apparent part of my professional life until I retired from it.

My relationship to Dr Barnardo's Homes, however, did assume some significance soon after my return from America, for I was invited to become a member of their Council. It was never quite clear to me whether the invitation arose entirely from my status as a relatively well-qualified specialist doctor, with some experience of caring for children, or from the fact that some of its members knew that I was an ex-Barnardo boy. I took it as the former, and tried to offer my particular expertise accordingly. The meetings took place in a magnificent room just beyond Coram's Fields – the part of London that I knew from my time as a medical student – and I enjoyed them. It was a body that inspired my respect and affection; I found the deliberations of its distinguished members thoughtful and wise, and I felt privileged to participate in them. I tried to contribute to them as a specialised carer, but the awareness of Barnardo's compassion that I had felt so strongly in his study many years before, was always there. It coloured my views, most particularly on one occasion when I took my turn as Council representative at an appointments interview for a member of staff. I raised some doubts about the appointment ostensibly based upon clinical observations, but actually originating in my own Barnardo childhood, for I felt that I would not have been happy as a child in her care. The appointment was made. Later I received advice from a member of Council on how to attend such interviews without interfering with the Management representatives making the appointment.

By that time the Council was engaged in altering the Constitution of the organisation, of necessity, I gathered, in order to meet the different needs of children by becoming a part of our modern social network. Phrases expressing Evangelical Christian and Church of England requirements had to be altered as too restrictive for both children and donors. I was inclined to be a dissenter in these discussions, more by feeling than by reason. Neither my Christianity nor my ethics had remained close to their Barnardo origins, and my form of medical practice became very different from his, but I think the kind of love which I received from my foster mother, from Miss Bristow at Euston Hall, from Gussy Duck and Pop Bailey at Russell Cotes, and even the good care given to me later by some of the staff at Headquarters, and from Mr Lucette in particular, emanated from Barnardo's compassion. His arduous loving had brought together other adults who had similar love, and children, like me, who needed it; and for this he fought.

By the same tokens, my own conduct in breaking up my first family was incompatible with being a member of the Barnardo Council, I thought, and on these grounds, I offered my resignation, quite fortuitously. The Chairman, a most distinguished retired civil servant, whose views I greatly respected, wished not to accept it, but I insisted. A number of members wrote touching notes of regret and appreciation, but none ever told me why I had been asked to join so distinguished a body. I believe I was the first Barnardo boy so to do.

Throughout the years of neurosurgical practice, I did not promote professional relationships through either private practice or medical social activities, and have purposely not shared my personal and family life with medical colleagues. I have remained relatively outspoken over most medical matters, but not on private issues. None learnt from me of the break up of my first family, and but one or two have shared in the joy and comfort of my later one. It is to the person who has seen most intimately my struggles of these last few years, and my more recent pre-occupation with my origins, that I remain forever indebted.

Master Weaver

This composition has assembled strands that I know to have been important to the life of an unwanted boy who was put into Dr Barnardo's Homes in early childhood. They have been followed as my life has been woven across them. I have presented the warp as determining the progressive accumulation of the weft. The whole, like a woven covering, can be judged by both its strength and its pattern.

Unlike a child with parents, who can put out tendrils to his constant supports, the orphan is carried relentlessly back and forth with the passage of time, attaching to whatever support he finds. These strands are the different people who have cared at different times, and to these he binds. Some impart affection, some shape an ethos, and some inspire emulation. He is unlikely to find the whole of parenthood for the whole of his childhood.

Dr Barnardo provided me with a number of these strands, both of motherhood and of fatherhood, to which I bound while they were there, and learnt to pass on when they were not. There was patchiness in the process, and I had to adapt; with less strands and less adaptation, I would have fared badly. Barnardo also imparted an ethos on which he based his compassion. This had a discipline, which I feared, and a Father, to whom I could only relate as a protector. But to whom do I attribute the remarkable opportunity I had as a Barnardo child? Again, it required adaptation as much as intellect to make use of it. Thereafter, Barnardo strands had others alongside, and when I most needed it, Fatherhood came closer, incarnate, but not really human, and my family a more universal one.

The strands across which I have subsequently plied have been more of my own choosing, and the weaving more in my own hand. Its strength may be that of a master weaver, but what of the patterns that can be seen? Some may reflect compassion, caring, and some gleanings from being loved may have shown in loving. Some may have the shapes of deprivation and shades of darkness.

Are these the patterns of a Master Weaver?

Acknowledgements:

To Anne for holding so much together over so many years.

To my daughters for remaining supportive.

To Clare, John, Hilary, and David, for careful reading.

To HBB for staying.

To Barnardos for updating so many Old Boys and Girls on their childhood in the last year or two.

To Dr Barnardo's Homes for remarkable graphic archives.

To Thomas John Barnardo for caring.

Printed in Great Britain
by Amazon

32357218R00116